ACTION SPEAKS LOUDER

A Handbook of Structured Group Techniques

A. Jane Remocker BSR OT(C)
Occupational Therapist, B.C. Children's Hospital, Vancouver, B.C., Canada

Elizabeth T. Storch BA OT(C)
Sole Charge Occupational Therapist, Greater Vancouver Mental Health Service, Vancouver, B.C., Canada

Foreword by
Lila N. Quastel MA OT(C)
CEO and Consulting Occupational Therapist, Northwest Rehabilitation Consulting and Management Services; Assistant Professor Emerita, School of Rehabilitation Medicine, Faculty of Medicine, University of British Columbia

FIFTH EDITION

CHURCHILL LIVINGSTONE
Edinburgh London Madrid Melbourne New York and Tokyo 1992

CHURCHILL LIVINGSTONE
Medical Division of Longman Group Limited

Distributed in the United States of America by Churchill Livingstone Inc.,
650 Avenue of the Americas, New York, N.Y. 10011, and by associated
companies, branches and representatives throughout the world.

First edition 1977, published by A. Jane Remocker and Elizabeth T. Storch
Second edition 1979
Third edition 1982
Fourth edition 1987
Fifth edition 1992
  Reprinted 1993
  Reprinted 1995

ISBN   0-443-04364-7

British Library Cataloguing in Publication Data
A catalogue record for this book is available from the British Library.

Library of Congress Cataloging in Publication Data
A catalog record for this book is available from the Library of Congress.

The
publisher's
policy is to use
**paper manufactured
from sustainable forests**

Produced by Longman Singapore Publishers (Pte) Ltd.
Printed in Singapore

ABOUT THE AUTHORS

A. Jane Remocker is a graduate of the Dorset House School of Occupational Therapy, Oxford, England, and of the University of British Columbia, Canada. She has 11 years experience in a variety of psychiatric settings and is presently working in paediatrics. She has been responsible for setting up programmes in an acute-care hospital and a daycare programme and is widely experienced in working with groups of chronic psychiatric patients and the elderly in the community. She has served as a consultant to community-based organisations working with psychiatric patients, and to the Canadian Association of Occupational Therapists.

Elizabeth T. Storch obtained her BA at the University of British Columbia and is a graduate of the Special School of Occupational Therapy, Kingston, Ontario, Canada. During her 28 years of clinical experience she has gained a reputation for being an expert in group techniques with psychiatric patients. She has worked with the physically handicapped and with psychiatric patients in acute-care hospitals, both in-patient and day care centres, in a chronic residential hospital and in a community treatment centre. She has acted as a consultant in nonverbal techniques for both acute and chronic patients, and has been a guest lecturer at the School of Rehabilitation Medicine, University of British Columbia and at the School of Occupational Therapy at the Central Institute of Technology in Wellington, New Zealand. At present she is a sole charge Occupational Therapist in a community-based mental health team and honorary Clinical Instructor at the University of British Columbia.

For Churchill Livingstone

Publisher : Mary Law
Editorial Co-ordination : Editorial Resources Unit
Production Controller : Nancy Henry
Design : Design Resources Unit
Sales Promotion Executive : Hilary Brown

Foreword

This little book is my old friend. I was a colleague of the authors at the time of its inception; I watched its growth and development, celebrated its publication and applauded its popularity. I have used it extensively with small groups of clients and introduced it to successive classes of occupational therapy students since 1977. The old friend has endured the test of time because it meets not one, but three of the four ends proposed by John Denham: use, wisdom and delight.

The book is for people who help people to help themselves. It is for mental health workers who understand the healing effects of both doing and talking. It is not true that actions speak louder than words. Each has an equal potential to be harmful or helpful. Together, doing and communicating can be powerful therapeutic tools, if used with sensitivity. The techniques described in this book encourage the use of a delicate interplay of both actions and words in delightful group exercises. The layout is cookbook style for ease of access and use. Each group activity is described in detail, including materials, timing, procedures and problems for which the activity is recommended. Like a valued recipe, once the exercise becomes familiar, variations and innovations present themselves for repeated use. The chapter entitled *Some basic concepts* is packed with information for students and provides good reference for educators and clinicians.

The wisdom of this book lies in the attention to universal, enduring mental health concepts such as self-esteem, trust, awareness of self and others, etc. The experienced authors write with clarity, simplicity and insight about those states of being when people become locked into themselves, self-deprecating and uncommunicative. To assist another person out of such a state is an art, a science, an acquired skill. My old friend endures because the authors had the wisdom to provide practical guidance in the development of such skills.

This book is fun to read and use. Many of the exercises help people laugh at themselves and with each other. Try a debate about jelly beans or log cabins; play the game of murder; or find out just who stole those cookies from the cookie jar.

For wisdom, delight and use, this is a wonderful handbook of structured group techniques. In this new fifth edition the basic format and layout remain the same. The authors have enlarged the content and included current concepts in occupational therapy familiar to students in the 1990s. I trust this old friend of mine will still be around, used and useful, well into the 21st century. Try it; it may become your friend also.

Bookes give not wisdome where none was before,
But where some is, there reading makes it more.
Sir John Harrington

Vancouver, Canada, 1992   Lila Quastel

Preface

When we first wrote this book in 1977 we were both newly married, energetic young professionals, with 21 years' experience collectively in Occupational Therapy. The idea for the book evolved out of our clinical work in an acute-care teaching hospital, where some of our time was spent instructing other professionals and students on the effective use of structured group techniques. The book in its final form resulted from the merging of our two different cultural and educational perspectives – Betty's from Canada and Jane's from England.

Our families grew; our clinical experience widened and significant developments occurred in the fields of Psychiatry and Occupational Therapy. In Psychiatry, for example, there has been an increasing emphasis on biochemical intervention as well as recognition of the need to treat each patient holistically. Patient populations have also changed due to a philosophy based on treating more people within their own community rather than in the hospital setting. Thus the patient population in acute-care hospitals tends to be more severely ill, whereas out-patient units and other community facilities are treating an ever-increasing number of chronic patients. With the growing importance of adequate social skills for the chronic patients and the rebuilding of self-esteem for the acutely-ill patients, structured groupwork is a valuable treatment mode to meet these needs. Rogers, in his paper 'Interpersonal Relationships: USA 2000', suggests that the small group experience provides a way of helping society to cope with an ever-increasing rate of change and is, perhaps, the most significant social intervention of the century.*

The profession of Occupational Therapy has developed a clearer definition of its role in assessment and treatment in Psychiatry. Assessment now is focused not merely on problems and strengths, but also on the underlying causes.

In this fifth edition we have described two current paradigms of Occupational Therapy, one developed by Gary Kielhofner and the other by Gail Fidler, both occupational therapists from the United States. Kielhofner's Model of Human Occupation and Fidler's Lifestyle Performance Model represent different methods of assessing and treating a patient's functional state, using a specific frame of reference.

---

* Rogers, C. R. (1968) *Interpersonal Relationships: USA 2000*. Journal of Applied Behavioural Science 4: 265–280.

We hope that the presentation of these models in the context of structured groupwork will make them easier to understand. Once understood, we believe our readers will be able to use these enjoyable exercises to assess and treat their patients within a theoretical framework.

Vancouver, Canada 1992

E.T.S.
A.J.R.

Acknowledgements

We developed *Action Speaks Louder* from our experience of working directly with patients, without whose participation and enthusiasm this book could not have been written. We were assisted and encouraged by fellow professionals. In the earlier editions special thanks were due to Shirley Salomon BSR(OT), Chris Morrant MB BS D(Obst) RCOG DPM FRC P(C), David Conlin MSW BSW and Ken Buhay of Encountering Theatre.

This fifth edition would not have been possible without the considerable input of Desirée Betz BSR(OT), who helped us translate part of the book into the language of current theoretical models; from Lila Quastel MA OT(C), for her advice, support and considerable encouragement in completing a difficult task; and from Tim Readman Dip COT PG Ed Dev OT(C), for final editing.

Lastly we are grateful to our families, Geoff, Ben, Sara, Gail and Chris, for their cheerful patience with us during the book's conception and successive rebirths.

Contents

Introduction

In this manual you will find a collection of exercises which have been designed to help individuals discover themselves and their feelings. The self-awareness which they gain will give them the strength to go out and not only meet other people but also experience more satisfying communication.

The exercises have come to us as folk-songs come to the balladeer. Some of them have been handed down from person to person and, as a result, have become changed. They are described as variations and appear as footnotes to the original exercises. Some exercises have been invented in order to solve a particular problem at hand and some have developed spontaneously from a previous exercise or from one aspect of a group's discussion.

We have compiled this book of techniques as a result of our own experiences working with small groups in a variety of psychiatric settings. These people, aside from their presenting problems, often seemed to exhibit one or more of the following general difficulties:

— inability to communicate effectively with others
— inability to recognize and express their feelings
— inability to perceive others and/or self accurately
— inability to generate more than an inadequate and limited number of solutions to personal problems
— inability to control the arousal of debilitating anxiety.

Historically, these people, often psychotic or extremely disturbed, were unable to function in high level group therapy. It was necessary, therefore, to develop a lower level psychotherapy group, one which addressed the real and special needs of these people through structured activity. This type of groupwork, where activities are designed specifically to reflect the functional level of the clients, creates a therapeutic environment which identifies and builds on the remaining skills of each person, rather than on those which are lacking. In general, severely disturbed clients seem to respond better in these types of groups than in unstructured psychotherapy groups.[1,2]

We have come to realize, since we began using structured exercises, that this mode of working has a far wider application than to the

1. Smith, P. B. (Ed.) (1980) *Small Groups and Personal Change*, p. 111. London: Methuen.
2. Kaplan, Kathy L. (1988) *Directive Group Therapy*. New Jersey: Slack.

chronic patients with whom we began. This is because the exercises provide an opportunity for learning: learning new and more appropriate ways of relating, learning about oneself and one's reactions to situations, and learning about other people. The key to their effectiveness, however, is that they are simple and enjoyable for the participants. Although the exercises are written in a form that is suitable for use with chronic patients, they can be adapted to suit the age, level of functioning and purpose of any group of people who meet together in order to improve their self-awareness and ability to interact.

In the past, occupational therapists have applied a wide range of psychological theories to their practice. As a result of rapid changes in the profession in the 1980s, however, there has been a growing movement to define and articulate specific occupational therapy frames of reference that are distinct from psychological theories.[3]

Several frames of reference have emerged, representing the legitimate application of Occupational Therapy. Originally *Action Speaks Louder* emerged from the self-awareness movement of the 1970s and was loosely based on a behavioural model. This edition has undergone a minor metamorphosis to bring it in line with two of the more commonly used frames of reference: The Model of Human Occupation by Kielhofner, and the Model of Life-style Performance by Fidler.[4, 5]

Model of Human Occupation The Model of Human Occupation draws upon concepts from systems theory. It views every individual as an 'open system' in constant interaction with the environment. How the person functions is determined by the state of his internal organization and external environment, or, more usually, a combination of both. The internal organization of a person can be determined by assessing the three sub-systems of Volition, Habituation and Performance and their interrelationships. Assessment of these sub-systems must recognize that they are conceptualized as existing in a hierarchical relationship to one another.[6] The Volition sub-system is responsible for choosing and initiating occupational behaviour; the Habituation sub-system organizes occupational behaviour into patterns or routines; and the Performance sub-system is responsible for producing occupational behaviour.

Dysfunction of any one of the sub-systems can cause problems at another level. For example, ulcers are caused by an overstimulated para-sympathetic nervous system (Performance sub-system) due to patterns of overwork (Habituation sub-system) and high stress and competition in the workplace (Volition sub-system).

---

3. Denton, Peggy (1987) *Psychiatric Occupational Therapy, A workbook of practical skills*. Boston: Little, Brown.
4. Kielhofner, G. (Ed.) (1985) *A Model of Human Occupation, Theory and Application*. Baltimore: Williams & Wilkins.
5. Fidler, G. S. (1988) The Life-style Performance Profile. In Robertson, Susan G. (Ed.) Focus: *Skills for Assessment and Treatment*. Section: Frames of Reference – Practice Models. Rockville, MD
6. For example, Volition is constrained where deficiencies exist in the other sub-systems, whereas problems with Volition disorganize Habituation and Performance levels.

A person, however conceptualized, does not exist in a vacuum. By viewing a person as an 'open system', the Model of Human Occupation recognizes that an individual is in constant interaction with the physical and social environment. Behaviour is maintained or changed through the cyclical process of intake, throughput, output and feedback. An individual's actions are considered to be the output of the human system. Feedback is provided by the consequences of these actions and this information is received by the person as intake. Throughput has already been discussed as the person's ability to process information based on the internal state of organisation. For example, in the exercise *Soapbox debate*, each person in the group makes decisions about the chosen topic based on past knowledge and experience (intake); from this he then formulates and presents his ideas to the group (output); the response of the other group members, both verbally and nonverbally, will give information about his performance (feedback); feeling good about clearly stating his ideas to others gives a person confidence to express himself in social situations in the future (throughput).

Throughput can affect the three sub-systems in different ways. It affects Volition by reinforcing the individual's belief that expressing opinions is enjoyable, which will increase the likelihood that he will share his opinions with others more often. It affects Habituation because, having experienced success in formulating and verbalising his ideas, the view that he held of himself of not being interesting to listen to or not being able to think clearly becomes invalid, resulting in more frequent exchanges of ideas with his friends. It affects Performance because, as the individual formulated and shared his opinions socially, the feedback of what works and what does not is incorporated into the self-image that guides his performance, and his skills improve.

Treatment and the selection of suitable exercises are also guided by the principles of systems theory and are based on rules of hierarchy:

1. *Higher levels guide lower levels.* This means that when planning a structured group one should focus on the highest level, in this case the Volitional sub-system, by taking into account a person's motivation, interest, goals, self-confidence and values when selecting activities.

2. *Lower levels constrain higher levels.* Structured group therapy should be organized at the lowest level, which would be the Performance sub-system. By developing basic skills at this particular level, change can be effected at the higher levels of Habituation or Volition.

3. *Dysfunction affects all levels.* Structured group work should focus on all three levels by using the high levels to assist and compensate for lack of skills at the lower levels. For example, an individual who has lost some short-term memory (Performance) can, through an exercise like *Name game*, learn techniques for remembering names through association (Habituation).

The Model of Human Occupation is an excellent one to use in conjunction with the exercises offered in this book since it emphasizes the concepts of adaptive behaviour, change through action, the importance of social and/or environmental interaction and motivation.[7]

Model of Life-style Performance   In this model Fidler defines a person's performance as 'the ability to master roles and tasks of living that are essential to achieving social efficacy and personal satisfaction'.[8] The overall purpose of intervention, therefore, is to improve a person's performance in the areas of work, play and self-maintenance.

The model identifies four separate skill clusters:

1. Self-care activity
2. Personal needs satisfaction
3. Contributions to the welfare of others
4. Reciprocal interpersonal relationships.

It also presents a structure for organizing and identifying performance skills and deficits. Fidler suggests the information be collected through an interview tool called the Life-style Performance Profile.

The Model of Life-style Performance proposes four component systems of performance, Sensory-motor, Cognitive, Psychological and Interpersonal. Each must be examined in order to formulate a treatment plan, and acquisition of skills in any one of the component systems will be influenced by a person's age, cultural heritage, environmental demands and personal experience.

Occupational Therapy, using this model 'is conceptualized as the process of using psychomotor activity to elicit those adaptive responses that support and enable the learning of performance skill'.[8] In *Action Speaks Louder* the exercises offer an opportunity to practise psychomotor activity in an enjoyable and constructive way. Exercises should be analysed and selected for their appropriateness, which means that each exercise's Sensory-motor, Cognitive, Psychological and Interpersonal components are matched with each person's problems, strengths, values and ability to learn and change.

The book contains over 50 exercises, suitable for use in structured groupwork. By using these exercises we hope the reader will acquire the philosophy, experience and confidence which is necessary to create new exercises more suited to the specific needs of the reader's own clientele.

LAYOUT   The manual has been designed as a practical textbook for the student interested in expanding his knowledge of structured group techniques and as a handy reference book for the graduate therapist or teacher. It has been organized to be read and used as one would a cookery book and the essential ingredients, which should be considered before

---

7. Kaplan, Kathy L. (1988) *Directive Group Therapy, Innovative Mental Health Treatment.* New Jersey: Slack.
8 Fidler, G. S. (1988) *The Life-style Performance Profile.* In Robertson, Susan G. *Focus: Skills for Assessment and Treatment.* Section: Frames of Reference – Practice Models. Rockville, MD

carrying out the procedure, are listed under the following headings: *Recommended for these problems, Stage of group development* and *Materials and equipment.*

The layout for each exercise is identical and the following is an explanation of the various headings we have used.

Title. This is the descriptive heading which is designed to help the leader quickly recall the technique involved. For example, *Who am I?* is an exercise in self-awareness.

Time. An approximate time allowance is given. This should be of assistance in the planning of a session, since it is important to know whether to use one exercise or several during the time available.

Recommended for these problems. If the exercises in this book are to be constructive and appropriate they should be related specifically to the problems of the individuals in the group. The first thing to do, therefore, is to identify the problem areas and then choose exercises which relate to them. In each exercise the problems addressed have been identified and articulated in the language of two models of Occupational Therapy: Human Occupation and Life-style Performance. For easy reference the problems are listed separately for each model and alongside the appropriate sub-system, for example:

> *Human Occupation* *Life-style Performance*
> Perf. Decreased concentration Cog. Short attention span

The sub-systems of the Model of Human Occupation have been abbreviated as follows: Vol. (Volition), Hab. (Habituation), Perf. (Performance). The sub-systems of the Model of Life-style Perform-ance have been abbreviated as follows: Sens/mo. (Sensory/motor), Cog. (Cognitive), Psyc. (Psychological), Intp. (Interpersonal). Several different problem areas can be focused upon in any one exercise.

Stage of group development. Under this heading we have indicated the degree of closeness in relationships which we feel should exist amongst the group members in order for the exercise to be appro-priate. Whether an exercise is suitable or not for a particular group of people depends on many complex factors. The general statements we have made regarding suitability, therefore, should be used as a guide-line only. However, in deciding whether to use an exercise or not, we feel the amount of interpersonal contact that is required by the exercise and the amount of interpersonal sharing that the group can actually tolerate are very important factors.

Synopsis. Under this heading you will find a thumbnail sketch of the exercise itself, including the goals and means of attaining them. The synopsis is designed with two purposes in mind. Firstly, that you, as the leader, can assess quickly whether the exercise is appropriate and, secondly, that once you are familiar with its title, you can recall the procedure easily.

Materials and equipment. In this section we have listed those things that need to be organized or prepared before starting an exercise. The materials required for some exercises include the preparation of a list of topics. Where this is necessary we have compiled some suggestions and these are found directly after the exercise. The ideal setting has been indicated but this is a guide only.

Procedure. This section is divided in half longitudinally. On the left-hand side of the page is a step-by-step description of how the exercise can be presented. On the right-hand side of the page is an explanation of the therapeutic aspects of some of the steps.

Discussion topics. The discussion which follows participation in any exercise is an important part of the whole experience. In fact, the main purpose of some exercises is to stimulate conversation, which then allows a person to talk about his subjective reactions, hear the comments of others and consider how this experience relates to his daily life. For example, in the exercise *Masks*, if through the discussion an individual becomes interested in the difference between how he appears to others and how he feels, this information may be integrated into the belief system, resulting in new patterns of behaviour. In the Human Occupation Model this information is input, the integration is throughput, while the change in behaviour is output. In the Life-style Performance Model this awareness in the Psychological sub-system will cause changes in the area of the Interpersonal sub-system. Without a discussion, most of the exercises may appear purposeless to the participants and lack relevance to their problems. Under this heading, in each exercise, you will find a few ideas to present to your group members for their consideration.

Variations. We have presented the exercises in their most basic and, therefore, structured format. For this reason they will not be suitable for all situations or all groups of people. The *Variations* space is an opportunity to record personal observations regarding the effectiveness of a particular exercise, variations that could be tried and recommendations for the future.

In reading through the book and in carrying out the exercises described, it should be pointed out that exercises such as these will rarely be used in isolation. They are far more likely to be utilized as part of a person's total treatment programme which may include such other things as chemotherapy, individual supportive psychotherapy, occupational therapy and recreational activities.

Finally, the book has been written to be used as a practical manual. We anticipate it will give ideas, stimulate the imagination and provide a creative method of approaching problems. However, it is only a beginning and we realise that there are areas which are, of necessity, brief. The Bibliography at the end of the book has been completely updated and contains some excellent additional reading, together with books and journal articles offering many more ideas for structured groupwork. For example, additional Trust exercises have been summarized by Smith (1980) in his book *Group Processes and Personal Change*.[9] These books can be obtained from public libraries and, together with this handbook, will provide a firm basis for the reader to develop a larger and more personalized repertoire of exercises.

9. Smith, P. B. (1980) *Group Processes and Personal Change*, p. 143. London: Harper and Row.

Some basic concepts

When preparing and leading any kind of group session or class there are many aspects that should be taken into consideration. We would like to use this chapter to share some of the concepts that we have learned as a result of our experience gained from working with groups.

FORETHOUGHTS
Planning a group

It is a mistake to underestimate the devastating effects resulting from insufficient preparation. The group leader should prepare not only the equipment and materials required but, in addition, should give thought to the sequence of exercises or *menu*. Rather like a balanced meal, the session should consist of a beginning, middle and end and in order to do this effectively the following points should be considered:

The needs of each person. In any group, each person will have his own particular problems. These are the problems that you will have identified in your initial assessment. These become translated into the goals that the person hopes to achieve, or at least work towards, while participating in appropriate exercises. Whereas the Human Occupation Model refers to them as 'patient problems' or 'treatment criteria', the Life-style Performance Model refers to them as 'skill deficiencies'.

This is always the first thing to think about, because it makes it possible to choose a *focus* for the session. The *focus* will probably be problem-related but where possible should be expressed in positive terms. For example, if one of the problems is that most of the people in the group have a diminished sense of personal effectiveness or loss of self-reliance, then the *focus* of the session could be building self-confidence.

We find that a *focus* helps people work on specific problems and also gives them a sense of doing something which is both purposeful and constructive. Too often, particularly in hospitals, patients are involved in groups and required to participate in various activities without adequate explanation about what they might expect to learn from them. So they feel anxious and apprehensive as they leave a session, wondering what it was all about.

Presentation   Once the needs of each individual have been assessed and the skill deficits identified, thought should be given to the overall manner in which the exercise or exercises are to be presented.

In an in-patient setting structured group treatment is the most effective method of presentation.[1] In order to accommodate a fluctuating population of patients in various stages of acute illness, treatment groups tend to be more effective using a supportive psychotherapeutic approach which allows skills to be addressed in a single session. In an outpatient setting a psychoeducational approach can be used, as the patient's illness has stabilized to a large extent, and patients are in a position to commit their attendance to a series of sessions. This method of presentation allows for skills to be taught in a single lesson or in a course of several lessons and is a very acceptable approach for patients, referring professionals and the group leader.[2]

The level of group cohesiveness. It is quite difficult to ascertain accurately the level of group cohesion but this can be assessed by considering, 'How long has the group been meeting together?', 'How well do the group members relate to one another?' 'How comfortable are they in group situations?', 'Do they trust one another?', Do they take an interest in or support one another?' and 'Can they risk expressing their feelings to one another?'.

Consideration of the above questions makes it possible to determine which exercises are suitable, since each one varies in the amount of interaction and personal sharing that it requires. For example, if a group is meeting together for the first time, it is unlikely that the people in it will feel able to share intimate problems. It would be much more suitable to focus the session on *becoming acquainted* and to utilize some exercises which would help the participants do this easily. In general structured exercises, and particularly those with a nonverbal component, enhance warmth, trust and cohesion within a group, as long as they are used appropriately and in a manner which is acceptable to the participants.[3]

The varying levels of concentration. Every person in a group will be able to concentrate for a different amount of time. Assessing this variable will help determine both which exercises are appropriate and also how many to use. A person's concentration tends to improve if he is truly interested in what is happening and if he is constantly involved and stimulated. This can be achieved if he is actively doing something or if he is given a part in the proceedings. Therefore, in a group where the majority of people have difficulty concentrating, it is usually advisable to use several exercises and to choose ones which are active rather than sedentary.

1. Kaplan, K. L. (1988) *Directive Group Therapy.* New Jersey: Slack.
2. Lillie, M. D., Armstrong, H. E. Jr (1982) *Contributions to the Development of Psychoeducational Approaches to Mental Health Service.* American Journal of Occupational Therapy 36: 438–442.
3. Smith, P. B. (1980) *Group Processes and Personal Changes,* p. 144. London: Harper & Row.

The size of the group. Obviously this is an important factor because some exercises are more effective when used with a large group of people and others are more suited to a small group. For example, many of the *theatre games* require an audience component. Other exercises, such as *Eavesdropping*, would take too long if the group were large and everyone was to take a turn. We find the optimum size for a structured group is eight to ten people, including staff.

If the membership of a structured group is small, e.g. five people including staff, we have noticed in practice that the participants may become anxious and reluctant to attend. This is usually because they are unsure of themselves and are afraid of being forced to participate, thereby appearing either a fool or a failure in front of other people. With this size of group, *video-replay techniques* can be used to advantage since there is time available to record, watch the tape and use it as a reference for discussion.[4] It is also possible to adapt and structure an exercise so that it can be done with two or three people just as effectively as with ten.

On the other hand, if a group is very large, then it can be extremely difficult to help the quiet, withdrawn person to become involved. It is sometimes best to split a large group into smaller units, or structure the session so that the quiet members have an opportunity to join in.

Expectations, the group leader's and the participants'. These play a very important part in any group session and a leader should always be conscious of them. It is appropriate for a group leader to have expectations; but these expectations should be realistic and not cause anxiety amongst the group members. Whenever possible the expectations of both the leader and participants should be discussed openly, for even if they are not talked about they are sensed and will affect everyone. The other aspect of expectations is that, if they are not met, they tend to evoke a wide range of feelings. The group leader may feel irritated, angry or disappointed, whilst the group members may experience a sense of failure, inadequacy or anxiety. If the expectations of everyone, both the leader and the participants, are clear and explicit, then the format of the session and the experience gained as a result of it will probably be more positive and rewarding.

Once these aspects of planning a group have been considered, it is possible to put together a treatment programme that suits the needs of the individuals who will be participating, reflects the general functioning level of the group and is flexible. The flexibility is vital since it will allow the opportunity for the programme to develop in a new or unexpected direction initiated by the participants rather than by the group leader.

Choice of Exercises   When choosing exercises for a structured group the first consideration is the level of physical activity which is required. The exercises in the book fall into three types: warm-up, active or verbal.

---

4. See Section on *Video-replay techniques*, p. 15.

Warm-up exercises are techniques of short duration which help people who do not know one another to *become acquainted* and generally more relaxed. They are usually used at the beginning of a group session, but can be introduced at other times if it is appropriate. *Warm-up* exercises can be used to promote an atmosphere in which individuals can begin to look at specific problems in greater detail.

Active exercises are techniques which tend to promote body aware-ness, coordination and/or interaction of a nonverbal kind. Generally, the stimulation required to hold the individual's attention is external, provided by the group as a whole or by individuals within it. Since a person's resistance is often well developed when it comes to words, use has been made of various expressive media such as music, art and drama.[5] These forms of creative expression enable a person to say something about himself at a time when he is still unable to express himself in words. Many of the exercises also provide an opportunity for a person to experience situations which he might avoid normally. The exercises enable members to loosen up with more basic instinctual and physical forms of expression, such as in body rhythm, movement, or use of colour, and may allow them to find new aspects of themselves which they may wish to explore, develop or change.

Verbal exercises are techniques generally of a more intellectual and sedentary nature. They tend to focus on such skills as the ability to speak clearly and concisely, to recall past knowledge and to organize thoughts logically. Many of the exercises make use of words, both written and spoken, and are ways of practising more effective com-munication. In contrast to the *active exercises*, the stimulation required to hold an individual's attention must often come from within himself.

Once the individual group members have been assessed according to the frame of reference that you have chosen and having decided the level of physical activity required, you are ready to select the exercises.

Using the Model of Human Occupation, activities are selected for the level of arousal, exploratory behaviour, acceptance or achievement that is required to encourage active participation on behalf of the patient. The role, therefore, of the occupational therapist is to analyse the organizational status of all systems and sub-systems and to plan exercises that are meaningful and productive.

Using the Life-style Performance Model, exercises should be selected to provide an opportunity for the patient to participate in activities which will remedy or compensate for deficits and teach performance skills. The exercises chosen should address the specific

---

5. The drama exercises included in the text are usually referred to as *Theatre games*. These are simple, structured exercises often used by actors to improve their abilities to think quickly, to be spontaneous, to improvise, to speak clearly, to trust others, to work in cooperation with others, to concentrate and to be decisive. The emphasis in most of them is upon clear, direct communication, whether it be verbal or nonverbal, and if they are used well they offer an excellent opportunity to practise, improve or change social behaviour in an enjoyable and accepting atmosphere.

areas of dysfunction and recognize existing strengths and resources. The patient's readiness to respond will depend upon his age, cultural background, economic and environmental resources.

In order to assist you to plan an effective group session, the exercises and problems/skill deficits have been cross-referenced in the Index.

The exercises are grouped according to the sub-systems they address in the two Models (Appendices A & B). Warm-up exercises are indicated to assist with the selection and sequencing of exercises. For further clarification the sub-systems have been defined in the Glossary.

There are some specific problems that participants may experience which contraindicate the choice of certain exercises. For example:

— incapacitating side-effects of medication on an individual such as tremor, blurred vision, Parkinsonism and dry mouth (contraindicated would be an exercise such as *Simultaneous conversations*)
— individuals with low ego-strength but high *I.Q.*, i.e. those who are demoralized by their diminished ability to think and who feel 'put down' by being asked to participate in exercises which they feel are simple and childish (contraindicated would be *Newspaper quiz*)
— the over-active person who is extremely easily stimulated and has a tendency to interrupt or be disruptive (contraindicated would be *Movement and sound circle* or *Soapbox debate*)
— the suspicious person whose suspiciousness may tend to be increased by the nature of the exercise (contraindicated would be *Eavesdropping*).

Lastly, always choose exercises which you, yourself, feel confident and comfortable doing, since your own involvement and enthusiasm will tend to inspire the group members. The experience should, in general, be an enjoyable and worthwhile one for everybody involved.

Related exercises   Choosing exercises and combinations of exercises is a skilful task. No matter how far apart the sessions are, they should be structured so that each exercise and session builds on the momentum and gains of the previous exercise or session. Thus it is possible to plan either a daily, weekly or monthly programme that serves the needs of the group members and is a sequence focusing on certain specific and identifiable goals. For example, given the general goal to become acquainted, a session could commence with a *warm-up* exercise such as the *Name game* and continue with one or two other related exercises such as *Likes and dislikes* or *Introductions*.

Location and time   The next things to consider, when planning a group session, are where it should be held and at what time. Thus the participant can incorporate the group into his daily routine with ease, due to the predictable time and familiar setting. Whatever the location and time chosen, we feel that these two factors should remain consistent throughout the life of the group. Even if one plans to use a different location for a particular session it is far better to meet at the usual location and move on from there. This is particularly true when the participants are travelling from their homes in order to attend.

A few exercises lend themselves to being done out of doors and, in fact, being taken out of their usual setting, will stimulate the participants to perceive a familiar experience from a completely different perspective. An example of this might be the *Blind walk*. This exercise can be used indoors as a trust exercise in which a person explores his ability to lead and his ability to be dependent upon another person. Taken outside, this exercise can take on the added dimension of providing a sensory awareness experience. A person would become aware of the complexities of his sense of touch, hearing and smell and thus may perceive aspects of nature that he never noticed before. Three factors which make it inadvisable to hold a group outside are: (1) if the exercise requires considerable concentration, (2) if the group contains some people who are easily distracted, and (3) if the group contains members who are on medication which makes them sensitive to the ultraviolet rays of the sun.

Usually the exercise and the discussion period following will be carried out in one location. There are times, however, when this is not advisable, for example, when the energy level of the group is very low. If this occurs, a break can be introduced by moving to another room and carrying out the discussion over coffee and cookies. Talking while eating is not only easier, but also tends to unite a group of people and to help them feel more comfortable with one another.

Whatever facilities are available, it is important to remember that the suitability of the chosen environment will impact directly on the effectiveness of the exercises.

Space   The features of the space where the group is going to be held should be considered when choosing the location, since this factor can encourage or discourage relaxed interaction between people. The space can be considered from three separate perspectives: the fixed-feature space, the semi-fixed feature space and the informal space.[6]

Fixed-feature space refers to the immovable boundaries, such as the walls, windows and doors. Since these features cannot be changed it is important to choose a room that is large or small enough to do the group exercises in comfortably.

Semi-fixed feature space is that which is organised by the movable objects within the room, such as the tables and chairs. People tend, either consciously or unconsciously, to assign meaning to both the fixed- and semi-fixed features and respond accordingly.

When arranging the table(s) and chairs for a structured group activity it is important to consider the type of interaction you wish to encourage and how you wish the group members to be oriented, one to another. When the semi-fixed features of space are arranged so as to encourage interaction this is called 'sociopetal'. When they are

6. Hall, E. T. (1966) *The Hidden Dimension*, pp 95–105. New York: Doubleday.

arranged to discourage interaction it is known as 'sociofugal'.[7] The most sociopetal position for two people is when they are face to face, whilst a much less sociopetal position is when they stand side by side at 180° to one another. For most group activities we prefer either the first position or somewhere between the two, such as is achieved by sitting group members in a circle, so they can see every other member without too much effort.

If the activity requires that a table or tables be used, the arrangement of the group members around the table can foster or inhibit interaction. Figure 1 shows a table arrangement for eight people. When such a seating plan is used the person at the 'head' of the table usually emerges as the leader. Consider whether you as the group leader wish to take this position or perhaps assign it to a group member whom you wish to encourage to take a leadership role. In a seating arrangement such as this there are also 'hot spot seats' where the participants tend to talk more. The two ends of the table and the two middle positions generate participation so that the amount of participation by each individual can be influenced to some degree by where he sits.[8]

Fig. 1

If you observe people in different social situations you will notice that they tend to choose different seating arrangements for different types of interaction. For comfortable conversation people like to sit at the corner of a table (Fig. 2a). If two people are working together on a task the side-by-side position is one they prefer (Fig. 2b), whereas, in competitive tasks, the participants often choose to sit across from one another (Fig. 2c).

7. Barnhart, S. A. (1976) *Introduction to Interpersonal Communication*, p. 95. New York: Thomas Y. Crowell.
8. Harrison, R. P. (1974) *Beyond Words: an introduction to nonverbal communication*, p. 153. New Jersey: Prentice Hall.

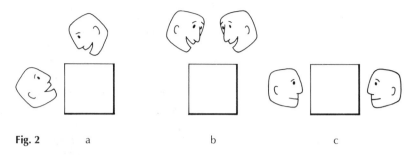

Fig. 2   a   b   c

Many structured group exercises suggest a more informal seating arrangement. Placing the chairs in a circle (Fig. 3a) or horseshoe arrangement (Fig. 3b) is a suitable solution. In the first arrangement each position encourages an equal amount of participation and the leader's position is not emphasised. In the horseshoe the leader sits slightly apart and, thereby, emphasises his position of control.[9] Organising the seating arrangement is, therefore, a very important part of the preparation of structured groups.

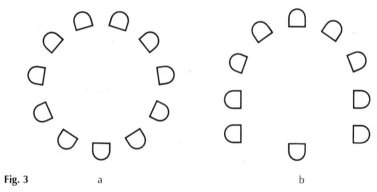

Fig. 3   a   b

The third kind of space to be considered is informal space. This is the space that surrounds each person. It can be thought of as a 'bubble' of air, the size of which varies for each one of us and for every different situation in which we find ourselves. It has been determined that each cultural group uses specific distances for specific types of interaction and that these vary between cultures.[10] When introducing exercises that require the participants to be physically close, be aware that for some the invasion of their personal space may cause considerable anxiety. An example is the exercise *Mirrors*. Some people can maintain eye-contact while standing very close, whereas others find it makes them feel uncomfortable but will manage the exercise if they can back away to a comfortable distance.

Video-replay techniques   Watching television is a common pastime for many people, making video television a familiar and acceptable medium to introduce into

9. Harrison, R. P. (1974) *Beyond Words: an introduction to nonverbal communication*, p. 154. New Jersey: Prentice Hall.
10. Barnhart, S. A. (1976) *Introduction to Interpersonal Communication*, p. 97. New York: Thomas Y. Crowell Co.

structured groupwork.[11] Its potential use is vast, limited really only by the availability and type of equipment and the creativity of the group leader. Some of the exercises in this manual are suitable for videotaping and, where we consider this to be so, we have included a footnote to this effect.

Taping a session can be done to provide the group with a visual and auditory record of the time they spent together. The tape can also be used as a very effective method of personal evaluation since the replay provides each person with an opportunity to look objectively at his or her own behaviour and to identify ineffective coping behaviours or defence mechanisms.[12]

We have used audio-visual replay techniques very successfully with exercises such as the ones in this book. Our experience, however, is that patients are often very anxious when the idea of taping a session is first brought up. We have learned, therefore, to introduce video-replay initially with exercises that are light-hearted (e.g. *theatre games* such as *Action mime, Hand puppets, The matchbox* or *Simultaneous conversations*). The action and replay of these exercises is usually entertaining and does not necessarily have to be analysed. If the video-replay techniques are used with care and sensitivity then they can be extremely rewarding and informative for all the participants.

Video can also be used successfully as an instructional tool. Many patients have inadequate skills for coping with emotional states and feelings.[13] Tapes can be used very effectively to present scenarios to which the individual can respond and for teaching more appropriate ways of responding.

Social functioning in the community can be taught using the medium of video. A variety of public employees, such as bus drivers, policemen, shopkeepers, social workers, etc. can be taped in their place of employment engaged in a typical dialogue with someone. Group members can view the interaction and practise questions and appropriate responses suitable for using in the community. Basic social skills, such as ritual greetings, how to begin and end conversations, how to give and receive compliments, etc. can also be shown using video. Role-playing situations or structured exercises can be used to reinforce learning.[14]

The medium of video-tape can also be used creatively. The making of a video-tape can provide an opportunity for the mastery of many skills and for expressing ideas. This approach has been used very successfully with adolescents.[15]

11. Goldstein, N., Collins, T. (1982) *Making Videotapes: An activity for hospitalised adolescents.* American Journal of Occupational Therapy 36: 530–533.
12. Holm, M. B. (1983) *Video as a medium in Occupational Therapy.* American Journal of Occupational Therapy 37: 531–534.
13. Denton, P. L. (1982) *Teaching interpersonal skills with videotape.* Occupational Therapy in Mental Health 2: 17
14. Holm, M. B. (1983) *Video as a medium in occupational therapy.* American Journal of Occupational Therapy 37: 531–534.
15. Goldstein, N., Collins, T. (1982) *Making Videotapes: An activity for hospitalised adolescents.* American Journal of Occupational Therapy 36: 530–533.

It is important for the therapist using video-replay to be very familiar with the equipment and its operation. This is because it is impossible to lead a group session calmly and perceptively if one is flustered and without half the necessary bits and pieces. It is also very important when using video-replay to ascertain from the group members that they are willing to have their group session taped.

THOUGHTS DURING THE SESSION

Opening the group

Open each session with the name of the group, e.g. 'Good morning, this is the Social Skills Group', so as to orientate those members who are confused and not quite ready to concentrate on the exercise at hand. Then introduce yourself and your co-therapist and ask the members in turn to introduce themselves. Or, if there is only one new member joining the group, ask the members to introduce themselves to him. Following this, give a few statements to introduce the general theme and explain the purpose of the specific exercises. It ensures that the session gets off to a good start by alleviating the initial apprehension that most people attending are likely to experience and helps the group members consider why they are there and what they might hope to learn. The introduction reinforces the importance of participating actively in the exercises.

Structured groupwork provides an experiential and enjoyable process, which is the essence of learning and behavioural change. Participation in purposeful activity is an effective aspect of a patient's treatment plan.

It can be advantageous to select one theme for an entire week and then to tailor the choice of exercises accordingly. If this is done, then introduce the theme at the first session of the week together with an explanation of the general purpose of the group. The latter will be beneficial for new members and is a task that can often be carried out very effectively by someone who attended during the previous week.

Presenting the exercise

The method of presentation can, and should, be varied, depending on the purpose of the exercise and the needs of the people in the group. For example, a group of students in a training session would need a far less simplified explanation than a group of young children or very withdrawn patients.

The therapist should begin by stating clearly the procedure and purpose of the exercise. When giving instructions, it is important to be aware of making them as explicit and concise as possible. The therapist should always enquire before commencing the exercise if everyone has understood the instructions correctly and be prepared to re-state specific points if there was anyone who did not follow all of them. This will provide an opportunity for points to be clarified, and give the person who is unassertive a chance to say he does not understand a particular part of the procedure. Once it has been ascertained that everyone has understood the steps in the procedure, the therapist is then in a better position to assess everyone's participation objectively. The job of re-stating is best done by the co-therapist since he, as a listener, is probably more conscious of any ambiguity.

The leader must know the directions of an exercise well and present them in a positive, assured manner. Some of the exercises may appear silly or childish if the group's confidence is not gained. They should be presented, therefore, in such a way that their usefulness becomes apparent (e.g. as a tool for greater self-awareness and for direct communication). The therapist should also communicate nonverbally with body movements to clarify instructions and invite people to take part in the exercise.

The leader can explain the purpose of an exercise when introducing it by name (e.g. 'We are going to do an exercise to help you feel more comfortable expressing yourself in front of others, called *The chair.*'). However, often it is better to move quickly from one exercise to another without any explanation in order to maintain the energy momentum. As the leader you must know the purpose of each exercise, but allow the participants to experience each one spontaneously without any pre-judgement. A discussion can always be held afterwards.

Roles   One important issue which determines the success of a group session is the whole question of leadership and roles.

Initially, leadership is usually assumed by the therapist or teacher. If you are working with another staff member, that person becomes your co-therapist. Both the leader and the co-therapist need to be actively involved in structured groupwork. For example, they should:

— participate fully in all parts of an exercise, acting as role models;
— volunteer personal information which is relevant to an exercise, enabling the group members to perceive them as people and to get to know them better;
— be ready to volunteer ideas if the group members are passive;
— be aware of everyone in the group and prepared to assist them individually to participate;
— be ready to move on to another exercise at any time if the group members become restless or lose interest;
— avoid sitting next to each other;
— lead the discussion following an exercise, having given consideration to the focus and how it can be related to the daily lives of the patients;
— encourage group members to make choices and decisions and
— be prepared to hand the leadership over to a group member or members whenever it is appropriate.

Sharing the leadership amongst group members can be achieved by choosing exercises which call for a series of leaders. For example, in *Movement and sound circle* the leader chooses another person to succeed him, in *Word circle* the leadership is taken over by the person who loses the game and in *Mirrors* the leadership is alternated between partners.

It is also very important to allow individuals as many opportunities as possible to make decisions within the group setting. The reason for this is that it has been shown that this can affect both self-perception and a sense of competency in a positive manner.[16]

During exercises which are primarily verbal, such as *Simultaneous conversations*, and during any of the discussion periods, the leader and co-therapist have these additional duties: to *equalize*, to *focus* and to *link-up*.

To *equalize* is to assist everyone to participate more or less equally. This means that the therapist must first become aware not only of those in the group who tend to monopolise the conversation but also of those who quietly withdraw from it. He must then attempt to bring the quiet people into the conversation, using the topic as a means of entry. The therapist can re-channel the comments of those who are tending to monopolise by repeating or re-stating what the talkative person has said. Then the therapist can relate it to the topic and direct a question to one of the quieter members, thus inviting him to take part.

To *focus* is to be aware of the topic at all times and to help the group members from being sidetracked.

To *link-up* the leader must listen carefully to what is being said and, where necessary, re-state what one person has said to another person, pointing out where their ideas or experiences are similar. The purpose is to help the participants learn to listen and talk to one another, rather than always directing their comments to you, the therapist. The leader must be careful not to monopolise the conversation. A recent study with chronic schizophrenics suggests that person to person interaction may be altered to some degree by the amount of prompting done by the group leader. The results of this study indicated that if the group leader delays prompting group members by about 10–15 seconds, this will in turn encourage the members to prompt one another.[17]

Leadership behaviour

There is a good deal of evidence that leaders of groups are highly influential. How does a therapist become an effective leader and what are the components of behaviour that contribute to that effectiveness?[18]

Lieberman et al. (1973) in their research concluded that four attributes of leader behaviour were identifiable. These were *emotional stimulation*, *caring*, *meaning attribution* and *executive function*. *Emotional stimulation* describes leader behaviour which emphasises revealing feelings, confrontation and challenging by both the leader and the group members. *Caring* refers to the giving of genuine praise,

16. Henry, A. D., Nelson, D. L., Duncombe, L. W. (1981) *Choice-making in Group and Individual activities.* American Journal of Occupational Therapy 38: 245–251.
17. Turvey, A. A., Main C. J., McCartney, A. (1985) *Social Activity Groups with Chronic Schizophrenics: the influence of the therapist's behaviour.* British Journal of Occupational Therapy 48: 302–304.
18. Smith, P. B. (Ed.) (1980) *Group Processes and Personal Change*, pp 81–100. London: Harper and Row.

affection and support in order to foster positive feedback between group members during the exercises. Throughout the session acknowledge the positive contributions of group members to help them feel valued. *Meaning attribution* involves interpreting behaviour and providing frameworks for change, whereas *executive function* is defined in terms of such behaviours as setting goals or directions of movement, managing time, questioning, interceding, setting limits and encouraging decision-making.[19]

Results of research as to which components of leadership behaviour are most important are not conclusive; however, all authors agree that an element of support and caring is essential. Within the framework of structured groupwork this aspect of being a leader is particularly necessary[20] whereas *emotional stimulation*, with its attendant confrontation, should be emphasised the least. The nature of structured activities inevitably involves the leader in a great deal of organising (executive function), particularly before the group meets. The activities themselves, if carefully chosen, tend to provide the medium for *meaning attribution*.

Many of the skills most strongly required of a good group leader are those very skills which are learned through experiences in groups. Thus it is suggested that the novice group leader should participate as a member in a variety of groups, seminars and discussions in order to develop a personal understanding of the group experience.[21] Working as a co-leader with an experienced leader, observing groups led by others and being observed leading groups, together with the all-important follow-up discussions about what occurred are also excellent ways to develop an effective leadership style.[22]

Sharing of feelings   Most people have some difficulty sharing their personal experiences in a group setting. There are various ways in which a therapist can make this easier for everyone concerned. For example, the people participating may feel more relaxed about talking if they are sitting around a small table, or are seated in a small room on some comfortable cushions talking over a cup of coffee.[23]

It is important for the therapist to act as a role-model by being prepared not only to participate in exercises but also to share some aspects of his own experiences. It is necessary only to relate information that you are comfortable sharing and, where possible, to express your precise feelings briefly rather than enter into a descriptive story of events and thoughts. No doubt some people will question the rationale behind this statement, maintaining that a therapist should remain uninvolved if he is to be effective. This is definitely

19. Lieberman, M. A., Yalom, I. D., Miles, M. B. (1973) *Encounter Groups: First Facts.* New York: Basic Books.
20. Smith, P. B. (Ed.) (1980) *Small Groups and Personal Change*, p. 113. London: Methuen.
21. Smith, P. B. (1980) *Group Processes and Personal Change*, pp. 81–100.
22. Ibid., pp. 198–205.
23. Bergel, E. E. (1955) Theory of Commensalism. *Urban Sociology*, p. 181. New York: McGraw-Hill.

true in some circumstances; however, in our experience this model is not true when utilizing exercises such as these. Remaining uninvolved not only reinforces the thought 'He's the therapist, I'm only the patient,' or 'He's the teacher, I'm only the student,' but it also impedes easy communication. By joining in, the therapist adds credibility to the exercise, enables the people in the group to relate to one another on a more equal basis and encourages more direct and open communication.

From our experience we have found that it is not advisable to force a person to share his feelings or reactions. Everyone has the right to contribute or withhold information and this should be respected. If the situation is not forced initially, a person is far more likely to share his ideas and feelings later on.

Subdividing a group　　In some exercises the therapist has the choice of asking people to work in *teams*, in *pairs* or *on their own*. Division of a group into smaller units must be done with sensitivity and care, and there are many ways of going about it.

Teams. A team is a group of people who may or may not have a leader but who have a common purpose. Teams tend to be competitive, and can effect the following responses:

— increased motivation to participate
— increased involvement
— cooperation between members
— a sense of unity within the team because of a common opponent
— enthusiasm and goal directed activity
— a sense of belonging to a smaller defined group.

A team is usually smaller in size than the regular group, which means that there are fewer people to relate to at any one time. This can be advantageous for the person who has great difficulty becoming involved with others.

Traditionally teams are formed by asking two people to be leaders and to choose their team members from the group. We find this method has very little value when working with people whose self-esteem is low, as the more popular members are chosen first, leaving someone with the feeling of rejection by being chosen last. Perhaps the simplest and most efficient method is to number off the participants 'one, two, one, two' and then ask them to form a team with all the other number ones, or number twos respectively. One can also arbitrarily split a group according to seating arrangement into smaller units. The last way, if you do not wish to use any of the above methods of team formation, is to leave the initiative to the group. Suggest they form into two equal teams with an even number of men and women on each.

Pairs. A pair is two people who are associated together. The situation where one person must work closely with another person during part of an exercise has many positive aspects:

— joint decision-making
— direct interaction with a specific person
— mutual support and ideas
— cooperation
— the sharing of information, experiences and feelings
— caring or taking responsibility for someone specific.

For the person who is very uncomfortable relating to a group of people, providing an opportunity in which he can start by relating to just one person is an excellent beginning. Two people constitute the smallest group and this tiny unit can always be enlarged slowly by structuring the situation (e.g. each pair joins another pair to make a foursome, and so on, until the whole group is reformed).

To divide a group into pairs one can invite each person to pair up with the person next to them, or give specific instructions such as 'Choose the person whom you feel you know best to be your partner'[24] or 'Choose the person whom you know least to be your partner'.[25]

Individuals. A person on his own can be very strong or very vulnerable. Many of the people we see in hospitals are often extremely isolated. They have withdrawn from society and exist without much contact with others. An exercise in which someone participates on his own for part of the time is aimed at helping him see his potential as an individual in relation to those around him. Choose exercises carefully so that each person can participate as best he can, without feeling a failure. Avoid pointing out a person's weaknesses in front of others, since he is probably well aware of them already. Instead, concentrate on assisting him to acknowledge his strengths. Working on one's own can offer the following opportunities:

— to see one's ideas put into effect
— to make decisions
— to take on responsibility
— to share and care for others
— to lead
— to look objectively at oneself, both strengths and weaknesses
— to improve skills
— to experience success
— to become more self-confident
— to realize the effect of one's actions upon others.

In summary then, whether you choose to have the group members work alone, in pairs or in teams, make this decision on the basis of their needs and abilities.

The discussion period   The discussion following an exercise is an important time. It is an opportunity to discuss something that has just happened and to begin putting the feelings experienced into words. The problems that a

24. Appropriate to use for the exercise *Blind walk*, p. 37.
25. Appropriate to use for the exercise *Introductions*, p. 70.

patient encounters during an exercise are often similar to those he experiences during his daily life. The discussion can be used to look more objectively at these difficulties.

The role of the therapist during the discussion is to have some questions prepared to stimulate conversation and to assist the members in expressing their experiences and feelings during the exercise.

Closing the group Most groups are quite lively, requiring a high degree of physical and emotional involvement. After the last exercise it is important to bring the group together once more, both physically and mentally. Ask the members to re-form into one group, then summarize the theme for that day and indicate the key points that emerged from the exercises. Then ask the group to reflect for a moment on the session; the experience they have had and its value to them. After a brief quiet period invite each person to share his thoughts. Close the group on a positive note by describing briefly the topic for the next meeting and reminding everyone of the date, time and location.

AFTERTHOUGHTS
Post group evaluation Once a group session is over, it is advisable to get together with the co-therapist and other staff members. This 10 minute post-group meeting is the most advantageous time both to assess the group and to plan for the following session. During it, each group member, the group as a whole, the exercises used and any drawings or written material resulting should be given consideration.

Assessment of individuals according to chosen Model Throughout the exercises in the book we have listed, opposite the steps in the procedure, the usefulness of these steps in observing certain aspects of a person's behaviour. From these observations assessments can be made and some conclusions drawn about each person's progress.

When using the Life-style Performance Model, observations should be recorded under the four sub-system categories of:

Sensory/motor	Level of physical activity
	Coordination
	Spatial orientation
Cognitive	Attention
	Memory
	Orientation
	Formulation of ideas
Psychological	Mood
	Thought content
	Participation
	Expression of feelings
	Self-care
Interpersonal	Verbal skills
	Non-verbal skills
	Cooperation
	Leadership skills
	Communication skills
	Trust

When using the Model of Human Occupation, the Directive Group Baseline Assessment Form (Fig. 4) is a useful tool. It provides a guide for focusing observations and for indicating strengths and weaknesses in each person's occupational functioning.

DIRECTIVE GROUP
Baseline Assessment Form

Referral problem(s): #
S– (What patient said, characteristic statement)

O– PLEASE INDICATE APPROPRIATE RATINGS AND DESCRIPTIONS OF PATIENT'S BEHAVIOR:

Basic Components of Volitional Sub-system	No	Partially	Yes	Not Observed
• Patient identifies personal interests	1	2	3	X
• Patient demonstrates goal-directed behavior	1	2	3	X
• Patient demonstrates evidence of pleasure in activities, spontaneity, and anticipation of success.	1	2	3	X

Comments: (e.g. interests, goals, and motivation)

Basic Role Behaviors				
• Patient participates actively in each activity	1	2	3	X
• Patient initiates one task-related comment/or makes one comment at a time	1	2	3	X
• Patient helps lead an activity	1	2	3	X

Comments: (e.g. manner/content of interaction, affect and coping skills)

Basic Self-Maintenance Habits				
• Patient is dressed in street clothes prior to beginning of session	1	2	3	X
• Patient attends group on time	1	2	3	X

Comments: (e.g. appearance, response to time expectations)

Basic Cognitive Skills				
• Patient is able to stay in session for duration of group	1	2	3	X
• Patient is able to focus attention for at least 25 minutes	1	2	3	X
• Patient is able to follow instructions on simple tasks	1	2	3	X
• Patient is able to explain directions	1	2	3	X

Comments: (e.g. fine, gross, and perceptual motor skills, elaborate on cognitive skills)

A– Assess patient's adaptive and maladaptive responses, areas of basic competence, comparison of current performance with past history, environmental requirements necessary to elicit adequate occupational behavior at this level.

P– Participate in the activities and relationships of Directive group for at least one week to work on the following short-term goal(s):

_____
Signature and Discipline's Initials

Fig. 4   Directive Group Baseline Assessment Form[26].

---

26. From Kaplan, K. L. (1988) *Directive Group Therapy*, p. 50. Thorofare, New Jersey: Slack.

Evaluation of the group process

The group as a whole must also be evaluated. Consider first the predominant feeling in the group (e.g. *anger*). If many of the members were angry, did you recognize it in time to use exercises that allowed the members to express or accept their anger? Did you initiate a discussion to help them investigate the cause of this anger? If the cause was known but the solution not attainable, did you use gross physical movement to allow an acceptable display of this anger? If you should have a similar mood in a future group, what would you change in order to handle it better?

Then consider the participation of the group members. Did they take part or was there a sense of reluctance? Did they interact with one another or maintain their isolation? Was the energy generated by the group high or low? Did the group members lead the discussion or did you, as the therapist, have to initiate all the questions and comments? As a result of the work done during the session do you have a clear *focus* for the next group?

Evaluation of appropriateness of exercises

This is the time to refer back to the *focus* of the group session and think about whether the exercises chosen were appropriate or not. Ask yourself if the session met your expectations as well as the needs of the patients. If it did not, ask yourself why. Was it that you chose inappropriate exercises or perhaps the appropriate ones but in an awkward sequence? Did you spend enough time *warming up*? Were the exercises active enough to involve all members? Were they too active, thereby excluding some people? Were they too intellectual? Was the content too abstract for the majority of the group members? Had the group evolved to a stage that allowed the members to share the feeling material you were seeking?

Think also about whether you were sufficiently well prepared and if the location you chose was a good one. Were the exercises selected suitable for the number of people in the group and, finally, did you present the exercises in the most understandable way? If you can answer these questions you will learn from both your mistakes and your successes.

Evaluation of projective material

It is wise to identify any projective material produced in the group, with the date, name of exercise and any comments. This should be done following the group and saved for your records and perhaps for research use later. Material that the group members have produced can be displayed but only after you have obtained their permission to do so. These drawings or diagrams express, diagrammatically, some very sensitive areas in those members' lives and any wishes to keep this material private must be treated with respect.

Displayed drawings can often be used as a shorthand reference for yourself and the group members if the same subject matter occurs in a subsequent group. The picture will help quick recall of the information the group members conveyed. Group productions can also be displayed. This material gives each person a sense of belonging as it shows a joint effort, composed of contributions, representing the personalities of the members involved.

Planning future groups   The last thing to think about in the process of evaluation is the next session. As we have mentioned before, each successive group should build on the momentum and experience of the previous one. When planning the next group, therefore, one should consider if any situation arose during the last group which could be used as a springboard. Often the group members are just beginning to share their ideas and feelings freely as it is time to end the session. If through an exercise at the beginning of the next session you are able to reconstruct the same level of communication at an earlier stage in the group process you will watch your group grow quickly and the goals you had set out for it attained.

Group record   For your own reference you may wish to record the progress of each group. To be brief and concise, we suggest recording:
  (1) the date
  (2) the number of people who attended
  (3) the number of staff
  (4) the major goal or focus of the group
  (5) the mood of the group
  (6) the exercises used to obtain that goal
  (7) a good to bad rating scale of the success of each exercise with explanatory comments.

Individual charting   Often very significant material comes out of a group, especially from those members who become less inhibited when doing nonverbal techniques. This material should be recorded as soon as possible on the member's chart or file in a format that is compatible with your chosen frame of reference.

EXERCISES

Action mime (warm-up)

Allow up to 30 minutes

This is an exercise to help a person express his ideas to others. It can be used as a *warm-up* technique.[1]

Recommended for these problems

Model of human occupation		Life-style performance model	
Vol.	– diminished sense of personal effectiveness	Sens/mo.	– slowed sensory-motor output
Perf.	– impairment of interpersonal communication skills as indicated by social isolation	Cog.	– short attention span – poverty of ideas
	– decreased concentration (5 minutes or less)	Psyc.	– loss of self-reliance
	– deficiency in neurological skills as indicated by poverty of ideas	Intp.	– limited social interaction
	– slowing of perceptual-motor skills		

Stage of group development

This exercise is valuable to use with any type of group, from a newly formed one to a cohesive and well integrated one.

Synopsis

It takes the form of a *theatre game* where the players take turns to perform an action mime, using a small article as a substitute for an imaginary one. The object of the game is to guess the identity of the imaginary article from the player's action mime.

Materials and equipment

Small articles, e.g. comb, book, box, ashtray, pencil, etc.
Use a familiar and quiet room where there will be no interruptions.

Procedure

Invite the players to sit in a circle	This enables each person to become more aware of the others. It also helps to unite the group
Place a small article, e.g. a comb, in the centre of the circle	

---

1. The exercise is suitable for *videotaping*. The replay will give each person a chance to see himself in action. This is an excellent exercise to videotape for those patients who are extremely anxious about the image they present.

Explain the exercise as follows:

'In the centre of the circle I have placed a comb. In turn[2] each of us is going to pick it up and, without words, use it in such a way that our action gives it a new identity. That is, we *must* not use it as a comb, but as something else. Allow its shape, size, weight and texture to stimulate your imagination, and the rest of us will try to guess what it is from your action'[3]

To provide an opportunity for each person to express himself and his imagination in a nonverbal manner

The game requires concentration and some spontaneity. A suitable action-mime will be immediately recognized and thus give the player a sense of achievement, whereas an inapt one will not be. The player can then be encouraged to try alternative and more realistic actions

'Once someone in the group has guessed the identity of the imagined object correctly place the comb back in the centre of the circle for the next person to pick up'

The physical action of picking up or putting back the object provides each person with an opportunity to indicate nonverbally that he is either ready to take his turn or finished with it

Continue until there are no more ideas forthcoming before substituting a different article or going on to another exercise

Do not change the article too quickly if you wish to encourage ingenuity and imagination

2. Once everyone has had a turn, it can be useful to allow individuals to volunteer to play, especially if they need opportunities to experience decision-making and risk-taking in a supportive environment.
3. If ideas are not forthcoming, the therapist and co-therapist should be ready to act as role-models, by taking a turn first. This demonstration will also help to clarify the instructions.

Allow 1 hour Balloon debate

This is an exercise in public speaking.[1]

Recommended for these problems

Model of human occupation	Life-style performance model
Vol. – feelings of powerlessness over personal actions – inhibited self-expression due to decreased expectancy of success Perf. – decreased concentration (5–15 minutes) – deficiencies in processing skills affecting planning – confused thinking due to neurological deficiencies	Cog. – confused thinking – difficulty making choices – limited concentration

Stage of group development   A group that is just beginning to enjoy a sense of cohesiveness will benefit most from this exercise.

Synopsis   The group imagines that they are seated in the basket of a hot-air balloon which is sinking. Although each of them is a famous person, the only way to save the balloon is to lighten it. Thus, all but one of the passengers must jump overboard. In a short speech, each person puts forward the reasons why he should be the one to be saved. Voting is based on the content of the speech, and the person with the most votes is the winner.

Materials and equipment   Pencils and paper
Use a familiar room that is quiet.

---

1. This exercise is suitable for *videotaping*, particularly if the purpose of the exercise is to help patients practise more effective speaking. The replay can then be used to look at such things as:
    — whether everyone spoke loudly enough
    — whether they spoke to the group as a whole or only to a segment of it
    — whether they were able to keep everyone's attention
    — whether they were able to emphasize their ideas with gestures and facial expressions.

Procedure

Invite everyone to sit in a circle	To promote awareness of the group as a unit and of the individuals in it
Pass around the paper and pencils, inviting everyone to keep one of each	To encourage a decision on each person's part to participate actively
Explain the exercise as follows: 'Imagine that we are all seated in the basket of a hot-air balloon which is sinking rapidly. The only way to prevent the balloon from crashing is to lighten it. All but one of us must jump overboard. However, since each one of us is a famous person, we are given the opportunity to put forward any reasons why we should be the one to be saved'	
'Firstly, decide which famous person you would like to be; you can be anyone either living or dead'[2]	This part of the exercise provides each person with an opportunity to make a decision and be imaginative
'In the next three minutes, write down all the arguments you can think of why you, as this famous person, should be saved'	To assist an individual to relate his assumed identity to reality, and to encourage the use of his abilities to remember, reason and be innovative
When the three minutes are up, invite one person to be the *secretary*. His job will be to write down the assumed name of each person as he speaks	This is an opportunity to involve a quiet person in an active role
Ask each person in turn to stand up and introduce himself to the group, using his assumed identity, and share the reasons why he considers he should be saved[3]	To provide an opportunity for delivering a brief speech
Encourage everyone else to listen attentively and to make notes if they wish	To assist concentration and recall
'When everyone has spoken, a vote will be taken and the person who receives the most votes will be the winner'	
'The *secretary* will record the votes'	The quiet player now has an opportunity to take a leadership role in the group

2. The therapist should be prepared to give suggestions to those patients who do not have any ideas (see Suggestions at the end of the exercise).
3. The therapist may need to restate the reasons presented if they are very garbled. Not only will this make the person's presentation more successful, but it will also give him the feeling that he has been understood.

At the time of voting the therapist should remind each player that he only has one vote which he should cast for the group member whose speech contained the most persuasive reasons. Players may not vote for themselves

This exercises decision-making

When all the votes have been cast, the *secretary* reads out the results

---

Discussion topics
— What feelings did players experience while standing up in front of everyone and giving their speeches?
— How do players feel and react in other situations where they are expected to contribute to the conversation?

Suggestions for 'Balloon debate'
The characters chosen can be famous politicians, comedians, singers, film stars, writers, inventors and sportsmen. They can be people who are alive today or who have died.

Queen Elizabeth II	King Henry VIII
Albert Einstein	Darwin
Captain Cook	Shakespeare
Yehudi Menuhin	Caesar
Margot Fonteyn	John Lennon
Napoleon	Scarlet Pimpernel
Johann Sebastian Bach	Elvis Presley
Florence Nightingale	John Wayne
	Margaret Thatcher

Variations

Blind circle (warm-up)

Allow 15–60 minutes

This is an exercise to increase a person's conscious awareness of other people, using senses other than sight.[1]

Recommended for these problems

Model of human occupation	Life-style performance model
Vol. – distorted body image – egocentricity Perf. – impairment of interpersonal communication skills as indicated by fear of touching people	Sens/mo. – distorted body image Intp. – fear of physical contact – egocentricity

Stage of group development This is a good exercise for a group whose members need physical contact in order to feel closer to each other.

Synopsis It takes the form of an identification game where each person closes his eyes and attempts to identify one person who has made various changes to his clothing and appearance.
It may be used as an extension to the *Blind walk*.

Materials and equipment None
Use a familiar room where there will be no interruptions.

Procedure

Invite the group members to stand in a circle, without touching one another, and facing inwards	To bring the group together
Explain the exercise as follows: 'Firstly, will everyone please close their eyes'	

---

1. The exercise is suitable for *videotaping*. Watching the replay afterwards will show participants what occurred while their eyes were closed. The replay can also be used to assist each person to recall his feelings during the exercise.

'I am going to guide one of you[2] into the centre of the circle and ask this person to make various changes in his clothing, (e.g. putting on glasses, taking off a jacket, wearing a hat, etc.)'	To provide an opportunity for the use of initiative and to make it difficult for the participants to identify the person from his clothing alone
'Only the person in the centre of the circle may open his eyes'	
'He will then silently stand in front of each one of you, in turn, and . . .	To encourage personal interaction through the sense of touch
'with your eyes closed you may like to try to identify him'	To encourage physical contact with another person, especially the upper part of his body To increase the ability to recognize a person from his features rather than his clothes The therapist should observe the reactions of the participants and use these observations to assist any discussion that may arise later
'When everyone has had a turn at guessing you may open your eyes and see if your guess was correct'	To provide an opportunity for feedback with regard to the accuracy of perceptions
Encourage discussion in terms of any reactions that were experienced during the exercise, why some people guessed correctly and why some did not, and so on	To promote the sharing of experiences between the participants and to assist learning about oneself and others
Continue the exercise with a different person/ volunteer in the centre of the circle	Repetition will help to reduce anxiety and reinforce any learning that may have occurred

Discussion topics   — How did you feel during the exercise?
— How did you identify the players when you had your eyes closed?
— Did you like touching people?
— What part does touching play in relationships?
— Which of your senses did you use?

Variations

---

2. If the members are quite self-assured, an alternative would be to ask if there is a volunteer who would like to be in the centre of the circle (request a show of hands while everyone's eyes are closed and select one person).

Allow 10–30 minutes # Blind run

This is an exercise to increase trust and self-confidence.[1]

Recommended for these problems

Model of human occupation	Life-style performance model
Vol. – impairment of interpersonal communication skills as indicated by: difficulty trusting people social anxiety – diminished sense of personal effectiveness	Psyc. – loss of self-reliance – feelings of anxiety Intp. – limited capacity for trust

Stage of group development This exercise should be done with a group who know one another quite well.

Synopsis The exercise requires that a person walk or run across an oval (formed by the other participants) with his eyes closed. As he reaches the perimeter of the oval he will be caught, turned around and redirected.

Materials and equipment None
Use a large familiar room that has no furniture in it or where the furniture can be pushed to one side.

Procedure

Invite the group members to form an oval	This brings the group together as a visual unit and ensures that the distances walked or run are different
Ask if there is one person who would like to be in the centre of the oval (Request that the gap he leaves is closed up)	To provide an opportunity for someone in the group to volunteer

1. The exercise is suitable for *videotaping*. The replay can be used to look at how each person was able to participate and particularly at how he used his body in relation to those around him.

Instruct this person as follows: 'Close your eyes tightly and turn around on the spot until you lose your sense of direction'	To promote disorientation of this person with regard to his position in the oval and, therefore, increase the degree to which he must rely on the participants to look after him
'Then stop turning and walk forward trying to maintain an even pace'	
'As your confidence increases, quicken your pace until you can run back and forth in a relaxed way'	To encourage self-awareness and trust The speed at which the person moves will indicate the degree to which he feels he can rely on the group members
'Tell us when you have had enough'	To promote decision-making
Instructions to the group: 'When the volunteer (use his name) reaches the edge of the oval the person nearest him must catch him carefully, gently turn him around and redirect him across the oval again'	To promote a sense of responsibility for another person and encourage gentle physical contact with him To encourage concentration upon what is happening
Continue with another volunteer in the centre	To enable each person to experience the exercise if they so wish
Invite discussion at the end of the exercise	To assist the sharing of feelings, reactions and observations amongst the participants To increase self-awareness

Discussion topics

— What is trust and how does it affect our relationships?
— What does it mean to be responsible for another person?
— How does it feel to be responsible for another person?
— How do we react in situations where we are dependent upon other people?
— How do we react to situations which are unfamiliar?

Variations

Blind walk

This is an exercise to increase trust and sensory awareness.[1]

Recommended for these problems

Model of human occupation	Life-style performance model

Vol. – feelings of powerlessness over personal actions resulting in apathy
     – impairment of interpersonal communication skills as indicated by:
         difficulty trusting people
         social isolation
Perf. – difficulty interpreting sensory cues
	Sens/mo. – limited tactile discrimination
	Psyc. – apathy
	Intp. – limited capacity for trust
	        – limited social interaction

Stage of group development   This exercise is appropriate to use with a group whose members are acquainted but are having difficulty trusting one another.

Synopsis   The exercise requires that the group members form pairs and take it in turns to be led about a room, with their eyes closed. During this blind walk the person has to try to identify objects to which he has been guided (or people to whom his partner has introduced him).

Materials and equipment   None
Use a familiar room which has furniture in it.[2]

Procedure

Invite the group members to choose a partner with whom they feel comfortable	To initiate social interaction and decision-making

---

1. The exercise is suitable for *videotaping*. The replay can be used to show the relationships between partners. The tape will also record the subtle nonverbal reactions of participants which can be used as a basis for discussion.
2. Go outdoors to provide a different experience.

Explain the exercise as follows:

'Will each pair decide between them who is to be the *leader* and who is to be the *blindman*'	To encourage cooperative interaction and provide an opportunity for choosing either a dominant or a submissive role in relation to the other person
'Will the *blindman* close his eyes and try to keep them closed throughout the exercise'	This will provide him with the experience of placing himself in the care of another person
'Meanwhile, the *leader* will gently guide his partner around the room making sure that he does not hurt himself'	To encourage a sense of responsibility and protectiveness towards another person To give some degree of physical contact
'When you feel the *blindman* trusts you . . .	To help develop awareness of how his partner is feeling as expressed by body movements
'take his hand and guide it toward objects[3] in the room, inviting him to identify them through his sense of touch'	To increase the capacity for accurately perceiving things using senses other than sight, and to provide an opportunity for enjoying the world in this way

"INVITING HIM TO IDENTIFY OBJECTS THROUGH HIS SENSE OF TOUCH"

3. When the group has experienced and is at ease identifying objects, the exercise can be extended so that each *blindman* is required to identify other group members by touch. The purpose of this variation is to help overcome the fear of touching other people and to promote the idea that this can be a pleasant and rewarding experience.

'Do this for 5 minutes[4] and then change roles so
that the *leader* becomes the *blindman* and
vice versa'

When this part of the exercise is over, invite the
group members to sit in a circle[5] and share
their feelings about the experience

Discussion topics   — What was the difference between the dominant (leader) and sub-
missive (blindman) roles?
— What was it like to touch objects and people? What feelings did
this arouse?
— Were you able to place your trust in another person?
— Were you afraid of bumping into objects and hurting yourself?
— How did you react?
— Did you experience any sensations from the environment?
— What were you aware of?
— Did you sense how your partner was feeling? How?
— What characteristics did you remember about the people you
were introduced to?
— Why is it important to notice things about people?
— How does being observant help one's relationships?

Variations

4. The time limit is arbitrary, but should be long enough to enable the *blindman* to
   become relaxed and at ease, and short enough to prevent him becoming bored.
5 To improve confidence by providing the opportunity for sharing feelings firstly with
   one other person and then with a gradually increasing number, invite each person
   to sit opposite his partner. Ask the two of them to share their feelings and reactions
   towards the exercise with each other and then to invite another pair to join them so
   that the four of them share their experiences. Continue in this manner until the
   whole group is involved in one discussion.

Building a road (warm-up)

Allow 15 minutes

This can be used as a *warm-up* exercise; it is a massage structured to promote both relaxation and body awareness.

Recommended for these problems

Model of human occupation	Life-style performance model

Vol. – loss of awareness of body sensations
Perf. – impairment of interpersonal communication skills
     as indicated by social anxiety
     – deficiencies in neurological skills
	Sens/mo. – limited gross motor coordination
	     – decreased body awareness
	Psyc. – feelings of anxiety

Stage of group development   This exercise can be used with a group at any stage of its development.

Synopsis   The group members work together in pairs. The partners take turns to massage one another's backs.

Materials and equipment   None

Procedure

Invite the group members to choose a partner with whom they feel comfortable	As the exercise involves touching, it is easier to do if each person is working with someone he knows and likes
Explain the exercise briefly, giving a demonstration with your co-leader	This is to help alleviate the anxiety that some people may experience by letting them see the fun that is involved, both for the person giving the massage and the recipient
Ask your partner·to stand with feet slightly apart, to bend forward at the waist so that his back is horizontal and to support himself by putting his hands on his knees	

'This is a massage that follows the stages of building a road'
'First you need to pick off all the trees on the surface.' Demonstrate by making picking movements with your fingers over the entire surface of the back, shoulders and neck area

---

'Then slap on the cement. Do not forget to do the neck and shoulders where most tension develops' Demonstrate slapping with the palms of the hands over the entire back. 'Ask your partner if he would like it harder or lighter

---

'Now smooth the cement into place' Demonstrate rubbing the back surface with the heels of the hands, moving in circular patterns

---

'And, last of all, we must draw the centre line. Do this with two fingers' Demonstrate using the index and mid-finger and quite rapidly draw an imaginary line down the spine from neck to waist

---

'Do this three or four times, then repeat the procedure in the opposite direction, from waist to neck, and finally ask your partner which one he prefers. The former should be relaxing and the latter invigorating'

Each person's preference, i.e. whether to be more relaxed or to be invigorated can be used as an index as to how he is feeling that day

---

Ask the group to begin the exercise with their chosen partner, while you call out the various steps
Then ask them to exchange positions so that the other person can be massaged

---

Discussion topics   The best conclusion to this exercise is to open up a general discussion about how the group members liked the experience. Make it brief and move on quickly to a more demanding exercise, so as to make best use of the relaxed open feeling attained by most members.

Variations

Caboose

Allow about 30 minutes

This is an exercise involving physical contact, cooperation and the chance to experience a dependent versus a protective role.

Recommended for these problems

Model of human occupation		Life-style performance model	
Vol.	– limited self-concept	Sens/mo.	– limited gross motor coordination
Perf.	– depression as indicated by psychomotor retardation	Psyc.	– lowered ability to assess personal skills
	– impairment of interpersonal communication skills		– depression
	as indicated by social isolation	Intp.	– limited social interaction

Stage of group development   This can be used as a *warm-up* exercise but it should be done with a group that has developed some degree of trust. It is often useful when the group has become inactive (stale) in the middle of a session.

Synopsis   In form this exercise is a variant of *Dodgeball*. The players encircle two group members, one of whom is *it* and the other is his *shield*. The players attempt to hit the person who is *it* below the knee with a thrown ball while he is being protected by his *shield*. If they are successful a new person becomes *it*.

Materials and equipment   A soft[1] large ball
Use a room that has plenty of free space.

Procedure

Invite the group to form a circle	The act of forming a circle requires some cooperation amongst the members, which may in turn stimulate greater awareness of themselves and others
Explain the exercise as follows: 'We are going to play a variation of *Dodgeball*'	To aid in comprehension by relating new experiences to familiar past experiences

---

1. Many older women are afraid of being hit by a thrown ball: a soft ball is less anxiety-provoking.

'Instead of one, there will be two people in the centre of the circle'

To provide a comfort to those people who dislike being the target of attention

'We will try to tag the first person (whom we will call *it*) with the ball while the second person (whom we will call the *shield*) will try to deflect the ball and thereby protect his partner'[2]

To give an opportunity for each person to play one of two roles: firstly, the guardian which is a protective role and secondly, the guarded, which is a dependent role
Once the individual has played a protective role and found it quite easy he will have more confidence in his protector when he is *it*

'When *it* is successfully tagged he is out. (To tag successfully the ball must hit *it* below the knees). Then the *shield* becomes *it* and the person who throws the ball successfully becomes the *shield*'

The successful individual is rewarded for a strategically planned and well coordinated shot with the honourable position of protecting someone else. This is in contrast to regular *Dodgeball* where there is no reward other than remaining on the team

As soon as any member of the group shows signs of restlessness, either change to another game or stop for a discussion

Discussion topics
— What was the difference between the two roles?
— What were the similarities between the two roles?
— What is teamwork?
— Is teamwork necessary during one's daily life?
— If so, why?
— What effects do the players feel after the physical exercise?

Variations

2. It is much more difficult to tag in this manner. Team cooperation is needed to pass the ball quickly between players in order to catch the unprotected *it* from behind. This has the effect of increasing concentration, interaction and cooperation between the individual group members.

Comment cards

Allow 45 minutes

This exercise is designed to increase an individual's awareness of other people, while involving him in a social situation which is not stressful.[1]

Recommended for these problems

Model of human occupation		Life-style performance model	
Vol.	– decreased belief in self as indicated by low self-esteem – lack of interest in others	Sens/mo.	– slowed sensory-motor output
Perf.	– impairment of interpersonal communication skills as indicated by social isolation – slowing of perceptual-motor skills	Intp. Psyc.	– decreased interest in others – limited social interaction – loss of self-esteem

Stage of group development

This exercise is suitable for a group in which the members are only superficially familiar with one another. It is a useful exercise for the development of group cohesion and can be used as a precursor to 'Eavesdropping'.

Synopsis

Each person thinks of a word or phrase to describe each member of the group. He writes his comment on a card which has been taped to the member's back and the descriptions are then shared and discussed.

Materials and equipment

8 cm × 13 cm cards
Masking tape
Pens
Use a room with chairs.

Procedure

Explain the exercise as follows:
'This exercise helps discover how you appear to other people'

By pointing out the personal gain achieved through the exercise, the leader can more effectively gain the attention and cooperation of those individuals who have difficulty participating in group therapy

---

1. Created by E. Storch, 1980.

Ask some members to help you hand out pens and cards, and ask them to assist in taping cards to people's backs

---

'We are going to move about the room. As you pass each person, think of a word or phrase which you consider aptly describes them and then write it on the card on their back'

Physically moving forwards and among other people is helpful for those members handicapped by feelings of social isolation

With the card out of sight, the individual is able to receive comments anonymously

Writing anonymous comments is not so revealing and, therefore, less stressful

---

When each member's card has a comment from everyone, ask the group to reform into a circle. Then invite each person to read out his list of comments

---

Discussion   Encourage each person to discuss his feelings about the comments he received; then assist the discussion to develop into a view of how he feels about himself.

Variations

Describe a diagram

Allow 1 hour

This is an exercise to illustrate the difference between two types of communication,[1] that is, between a monologue and a dialogue.

**Recommended for these
problems**

Model of human occupation	Life-style performance model
Perf. – deficiencies in process skills as indicated by difficulty planning – difficulty initiating conversation due to loss of interpersonal skills – decreased concentration[2] (5–15 minutes)	Cog. – short attention span – difficulty making choices Intp. – limited ability to initiate conversation

Stage of group development

This exercise is excellent for a group in which the members are still unfamiliar with each other. No feeling of group cohesion is needed.[3]

Synopsis

One person is asked to describe a diagram precisely. The group members listen to the description and individually attempt to reproduce the diagram on paper from the instructions given. No questions or gestures are allowed. A second diagram is then described but this time both questions and gestures are allowed. The group members are encouraged to discuss the two exercises comparing and contrasting them.

Materials and equipment[4]

Tables
Chairs
Diagram cards (see sample diagram ideas at the end of the exercise)[5]

---

1. The exercise is suitable for *videotaping*. Afterwards the replay can be used to look at and discuss specific difficulties that the participants experienced in trying to communicate. The tape will also help participants recall how they felt at any one time.
2. This is an exercise where all the participants are involved actively, all the time. It is suitable, therefore, for patients who have a short attention span and who need constant stimulation if they are to maintain any contact with reality.
3. Patients with temporal lobe lesions are likely to find this exercise very difficult. It is important that the therapist makes an accurate assessment of how complex the diagrams should be for the participants to achieve success and yet be stimulated.
4. To promote a sense of responsibility, invite the group to prepare the room and materials.
5. To increase self-esteem, invite the participants to design their own diagram cards.

Sheets of paper approximately the same size as the diagram cards,
e.g. 8 cm × 13 cm
Pencils
Erasers
Sharpener.

Procedure

Ask the group members to sit around the table(s)	
Pass around the pencils and paper inviting each person to take one of each	This encourages each person to be responsible for his participation
Explain the exercise as follows: 'One person in the group will be given a card on which there is a diagram. Only he may look at it'	This provides an opportunity to experience leadership
'He will describe the diagram slowly and as accurately as he can . . .	This encourages succinct, logical description, attention to detail, accurate judgement and concentration. It exercises the ability to perceive a shape and translate that perception into words
'while the rest of the group attempt to reproduce this diagram on paper from the instructions they hear'	This exercises the capacity to form a concept from auditory stimuli and reproduce this concept in graphic form. It assists concentration, attention to detail and accurate judgement
'No one may ask any questions. Try to be aware of any reactions or feelings you may have while doing the task'	This promotes self-awareness especially related to feelings in a situation where the communication is one-way only. The therapist should observe the reactions so that she can use her observations to stimulate discussion
'On completing the drawing there will be an opportunity for you to discuss your reactions and ascertain how accurate your diagram is before we proceed.'	This provides an opportunity for heightening awareness of the feelings experienced during the task and will focus attention on the problems and/or frustrations inherent in one-way communication
Ask if there is a volunteer who wants to describe the first diagram and give him the card (if there is no volunteer the therapist takes this role)	This transfers leadership from the therapist to the participants
When the first part of the exercise has been completed explain the second part as follows: 'Another person will describe a different diagram'	This enables more than one person to experience being the leader

'Again each group member will attempt to reproduce this from the description but this time you may ask questions'

This will promote two-way communication. The participants will ask questions to clarify points and so experience the feelings that result from successful communication

'The person giving the description may answer the questions and gesticulate to clarify the point he is making'

This provides an opportunity to practise using gestures in addition to words

'Again try to be aware of your reactions and feelings while doing this exercise'

This encourages the participants to be more aware of themselves in a particular situation

When the task is completed to the satisfaction of the group members, invite them to discuss the exercise

SOME SUGGESTIONS FOR DIAGRAMS

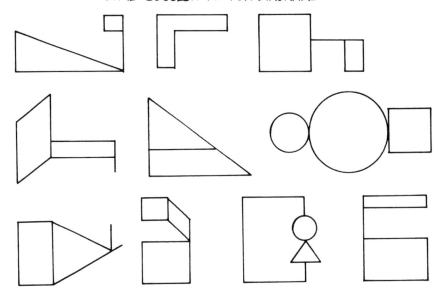

Discussion topics   Compare and contrast the two exercises considering the following:
— What feelings were evoked?
— How important were the gestures in aiding communication?
— How do these experiences (in communication) compare with our daily lives?
— Why is it important to be able to ask questions?
— Are there situations in your daily life which illustrate the two types of communication?

Variations

Allow 1 hour # Eavesdropping

This is a technique concerned with increasing awareness both of other people and oneself. It exercises the skills of perception, observation and memory.[1]

Recommended for these problems

Model of human occupation		Life-style performance model	
Vol.	– decreased belief in personal effectiveness	Cog.	– diminished retention and recall
	– limited self-concept	Psyc.	– loss of self-esteem
	– lack of interest in others as shown by passivity		– lowered ability to assess personal skills
	– decreased expectations of success	Interp.	– decreased interest in others
Perf.	– decreased concentration as indicated by forgetfulness		– limited social interaction
	– impairment of interpersonal communication skills as indicated by social isolation		

Stage of group development This exercise is suitable for a group in which the members know one another fairly well but do not give one another support. It is good for a group with low morale.[2]

Synopsis Each individual writes down everything he can remember about a group member who is out of sight. This person returns to the group and these observations are then shared and discussed.

Materials and equipment Sheets of paper
Pencils.

---

1. Created by E. Storch, 1972.
2. This is an excellent exercise to use when group or individual morale is low. The comments will, for the most part, be constructive and encouraging and result in the increased confidence and self-esteem of the participants. It should also be used in groups where the participants are very isolated, since it will encourage them to make some degree of contact with each other. This should result in an increased awareness of each other and more group cohesion.

Procedure

Invite the group members to sit in a small circle on the floor	This assists a sense of cohesion within the group and a relaxed atmosphere
Ask them to pass around the paper and pencils, keeping one of each for themselves	This encourages a decision to participate actively
Explain the exercise as follows: 'One person will volunteer to leave the room'	This allows each individual to decide whether he wishes to expose himself to comments from other people
'While he is away, the remainder of the group will each make a list of the things[3] they can remember about him (e.g. physical appearance, clothing, likes or dislikes, personal strengths, etc.)	This encourages increased awareness of other people. It means one has to think carefully about the person and recall facts, events, feelings, etc. pertaining to him
'When everyone has written all they can, the person outside the room will return and join the circle'	
Each participant will then be invited to read out what he has written down	This promotes direct verbal comment from one person to another. It provides an opportunity for experiencing the giving and receiving of supportive observations and constructive criticism
Discussion should be encouraged[4]	This encourages comparison of perceptions and an opportunity to clarify the feedback

Discussion topics — Do the comments compare or contrast with how each person sees himself?
— Why are the comments and observations of others important?
— In what situations does one normally receive comments about oneself from other people?
— How does each person deal with the comments?

Variations

---

3. This requirement can be made more specific, e.g. 'Write down all the problems that you remember he has.' At the same time, the person absent might list what he considers his problems to be. This would promote discussion, comparing and contrasting what the group see as problems and what the individual sees.
4. This exercise can be followed by a discussion of the types of things observed. It often happens that as the exercise progresses, the comments change from concrete observations of clothing, etc. to more abstract recollections of personality.

Allow 1–1$\frac{1}{2}$ hours # Expressions

This is an exercise which illustrates the part facial expression plays in communication between people.[1, 2]

Recommended for these problems

Model of human occupation	Life-style performance model
Vol. – limited self-concept – blunted affect – decreased belief in self as indicated by difficulty talking in a group situation – loss of self-esteem Perf. – decreased concentration[4] (5 minutes or less)	Cog. – short attention span[4] Psyc. – lowered ability to assess personal skills – flat affect[3] – loss of self-esteem Intp. – limited skills in verbal group interaction

Stage of group development   This is an excellent exercise for a group of withdrawn, depressed people. The group members need not know one another very well but some familiarity may be helpful if they are to work together easily.

Synopsis   The group members make a collage of faces, each one of which has been selected to show a different expression. The members then discuss each face and attempt to identify the underlying feeling or feelings. Finally, using the collage as a resource if necessary, each person mimes one of the previously identified feelings for the group to guess.

---

1. Created by E. Storch, 1972.
2. The second and third parts of this exercise are suitable for *videotaping*. When the replay is watched players will be able to see their own attempts at using their faces to express feelings. The replay will also bring into focus the fact that besides facial expression, feelings can be effectively communicated using body posture, body movements and gestures.
3. This exercise is particularly useful for patients whose faces tend to be expressionless and who are unaware of this fact. It can also be a rewarding experience for those who believe that no one can guess how they are feeling at a particular point in time.
4. The fact that the exercise is composed of three distinct parts means that it tends to re-focus the attention of patients who have difficulty maintaining contact with reality for long periods of time.

Materials and equipment[5]   A wide variety of magazines
Scissors
Glue
A large sheet of paper, e.g. 60 cm × 90 cm (on a separate table)
Felt pens
Small slips of paper and a container
Room which is large enough to provide adequate working space.

Procedure

Invite the group members to gather around the table	To encourage a sense of group cohesiveness
Give the following instructions: 'From the magazines provided, select and cut out a number of faces of people'	To promote active individual participation and exercise the capacities of choice and motor coordination
(Sometimes it is useful to limit the number of faces to be selected by each person, e.g. 2 or 5)	To give the participants limits within which to work and may help to reduce any anxiety arising through the tendency to be overinclusive. If the group is large and the attention span of the members short, this will also ensure that the collage contains a reasonable amount of resource material and yet represents each person
'Try to choose a variety of expressions'	To encourage discrimination through paying attention to detail as well as to assist recall of the wide range of emotions
'When you have made your selection, paste these faces on the paper to form a collage'[6]	To encourage goal-directed behaviour and cooperative interaction with the other participants
When this part of the exercise has been completed explain the next part: 'We now need two volunteers, a *leader* and a *secretary*'	To provide an opportunity for transferring leadership from the therapist to the group members
'The *leader* will select one of the faces on the collage and point to it. He will invite the rest of us to decide what feeling or feelings we consider the face is expressing'	This requires decisions by both the *leader* and participants, together with mutual cooperation. It provides a check for the accuracy of individual perceptions. It may also help to increase descriptive vocabulary and stimulate awareness of the range of feelings

5. To promote a sense of responsibility, involve several or all of the group members in the collection and return of the materials used and in the preparation of the room.
6. You can choose one or two people to paste the faces on to the paper. It is best if this job is given either to a person who feels cutting out pictures is beneath him or to a person who is restless. It provides an opportunity for leadership and making decisions.

'When the majority of us agree, the *secretary* will record this feeling on a slip of paper, which he will fold and place in a container'	To help the *leader* exercise his diplomacy and ability to recognize a final or majority decision
Inviting the group to gather around the collage, proceed with the exercise until all or most of the faces have been discussed	
Then remove the collage and ask the group to sit in a circle	This physical activity tends to promote renewed interest
In turn, invite each person to pick one of the slips of paper out of the container and mime the feeling written on it, for the group to guess[7]	To provide an opportunity for each person to experiment with the use of a larger range of facial expressions for which he receives recognition and feedback
At the end, ask the group members if they have any comments on the exercise	To encourage the participants to discuss the importance of observing and understanding facial expression as an aid to successful communication

Discussion topics — The ease or difficulty with which the participants were able to mime emotions.
— How any particular facial expression may affect others and thus our relationships.
— In what other ways do we express feelings nonverbally?

Variations[8]

---

7. Keep the collage as visual stimulus for those people who are unable to remember or mime a particular facial expression.
8. Ask the group members individually, in pairs, or groups, to find pictures of faces to illustrate some or all of the following feelings:
Boredom, trust, repulsion, relief, loneliness, hate, joy, anger, fear, contentment, strength, unfulfilment, support, confusion, shyness, inferiority, involvement, frustration, superiority, suspicion, attraction, hurt, love, sadness, affection, hope, weakness, satisfaction, rejection, or curiosity.
This would be valuable for patients who need more structure and/or whose descriptive abilities are severely impaired. It is a suggested variation. Discussion could be based on comparing and contrasting the pictures each group found to illustrate similar feelings or on the appropriateness of the pictures selected.

Feelings

Allow 1 hour

This is an exercise in self-awareness that focuses on feelings and their effect on relationships.[1]

Recommended for these problems

Model of human occupation	Life-style performance model
Vol. – inability to make decisions – limited self-concept – loss of internal locus of control as indicated by difficulty differentiating feelings Perf. – impairment of interpersonal communication skills as indicated by social isolation	Psyc. – lowered ability to assess personal skills – difficulty understanding and expressing feelings Intp. – limited social interaction

Stage of group development This exercise succeeds when some degree of trust has developed between the members.

Synopsis In this simple projective technique, the group members relax and determine how they are feeling. They depict this in an image on paper, then discuss it with the rest of the group.

Materials and equipment Chairs around a table
White paper
Coloured felt pens, crayons
Pencils.

Procedure

Ask the group members to find a comfortable position on their chairs, with arms and legs uncrossed and hands placed loosely on their laps	To reduce all external stimuli so as to facilitate concentration — images will occur more easily in this state
Suggest that each person close his eyes and try to relax completely. Then ask them to recall their predominant feeling during that day and how this feeling has shown itself in their interactions with others.	By transforming the feeling state into a visual image, each person is able to look at it in greater detail and some of the reasons for that feeling usually emerge

1. Created by E. Storch, 1985.

Then ask them to open their eyes when they feel ready, and put the feeling down on paper[2] in some sort of symbolic way. Explain that it can be expressed as a design, an animal or object, etc.

When everyone has finished ask for a volunteer to talk about his drawing. Ask questions about: 1. how that feeling affected the way he related to people around him; 2. if he felt others perceived how he was feeling; 3. if people or events altered his feeling in any way. Then ask the rest of the group in turn to describe their drawings

To help the person see more clearly that his emotional state does make a difference to others, and to see that it may trigger off some of the difficulties he has had in relating to others

"*I FEEL I CAN'T MOVE BECAUSE OF A HEAVY SADNESS*"

2. A variation of this is to ask them to shape clay to symbolise how they feel.

Allow 5–15 minutes # Find the change
(warm-up)

This is an exercise to increase the individual's ability to perceive another person accurately and to be innovative.

Recommended for these problems

Model of human occupation	Life-style performance model
Vol. – distorted body image – egocentricity – inability to make decisions Perf. – impairment of interpersonal communication skills resulting in social isolation	Cog. – short attention span Psyc. – distorted body image Intp. – limited social interaction – egocentricity

Stage of group development   This exercise could be used as an introductory exercise or, if the individuals in the group know each other well, as a *warm-up* exercise.

Synopsis   It takes the form of a game where two teams line up so that each player stands opposite a player from the other team. One team then turns to face the wall while each person in the other team changes three things about his appearance. On turning around, the first team must try to spot the changes. When each team has completed this, the number of changes can be increased.

Materials and equipment   Materials to keep the score.

Procedure

Invite the participants to form two teams of equal numbers[1]	To offer the experience of working together with a small number of people towards a common goal

1. Description of the formation of teams in the chapter *Some basic concepts*, p. 21.

Explain the exercise as follows:

'Would each team please form a line so that every player is paired off with and standing opposite a player from the other team. Stand about one metre apart'	To ensure that each person is standing in front of and reasonably close to another person, thereby assisting them to be aware of one another
Identify the teams (e.g. *A* and *B*)	To give each team a separate identity which encourages team spirit
Ask if there is a volunteer to do the scoring (if the number of participants is even, the therapist will need to take the volunteer's place in his team)	This provides an opportunity for someone who feels very unsure, or that the exercise is beneath him, to take a nonchallenging leadership role. Scoring introduces a competitive element to the exercise. Competition gives a sense of purpose and tends to encourage each person to try harder.
'Will each person on Team *A* take a good long look at your partner's appearance'	To encourage each person to look closely at another person
'When you think you have noticed all the details, turn your back on your partner'	This involves making a decision
'Team *B*, when everyone in Team *A* has their backs to you, each of you will change three things about your appearance'[2]	To encourage awareness of the other team and provide an opportunity to be innovative and subtle
'Let Team *A* know when you are ready'	To encourage cooperation
'On turning around, Team *A*, try to spot the three changes your partner has made'	To encourage verbal interaction and provide an opportunity for receiving immediate comments with regard to the accuracy of one's observations
Invite the scorer to record the total number of correct observations	To give this person an opportunity to interact with some or all of the group members
Repeat the exercise for Team *B*	

Variations

---

2. For example, undo a button that was done up, turn up your collar, change rings on fingers, and so on.

Allow 10 minutes (minimum) # Geography (warm-up)

This is a *warm-up* technique. It is an exercise which assists a person to think quickly, to concentrate and to practise immediate recall.

Recommended for these problems

Model of human occupation	Life-style performance model

Vol. – decreased belief in self as indicated by loss of self-esteem
 Perf. – decreased concentration (5 minutes or less)
      – deficiency in process skills as indicated by difficulty thinking quickly
	Cog. – short attention span
	      – diminished retention and recall
	      – slowness in thought-processing
	 Psyc. – loss of self-esteem

Stage of group development A group that is meeting for the first time can attain some degree of cohesion from this exercise. However, it is also enjoyable and useful to do with a group at any stage of its development.

Synopsis Each person in turn says the name of a geographical place. The name he chooses must begin with the last letter of the geographical name that his predecessor chose.[1]

Materials and equipment Use a room with chairs or a carpeted floor.

Procedure

Invite the group members to sit in a circle	To unite the group physically

---

1. This exercise is contraindicated for a group containing excessively active patients, or for patients for whom recall is so difficult that participation would be ego-deflating. People who do not speak English well can achieve success at this game, as they are not limited to English names only.

Explain the exercise as follows:
'The game begins with one person saying the name of a place (e.g. *London*). The person seated to his left will then give another geographical name beginning with the last letter of the previous word (if we follow the example, then the place name must begin with *N*, e.g. *New York*) and so the game continues around the circle'

To be able to take his turn, each player must concentrate on what the previous player says, assimilate what he heard and then express his own actual contribution clearly

---

'No names may be repeated'

This means that as the game progresses more and more names have to be remembered

---

'However, if a person cannot think of a name, anyone may give him a clue in the form of a question (e.g. 'What is the largest city in the USA?' Then he will remember *New York*)'

It is important, therefore, to encourage helpful communication between the group members and provide an opportunity (within the rules) for the restless person to participate when it is not his turn

---

Change to another exercise when you see signs of the first person becoming restless

Since this is a *warm-up* activity, it is best to stop while everyone is still interested and participating actively

---

Variations

Gifts

Allow 30 minutes

This is a simple exercise which facilitates a deeper understanding of self and a positive interaction with each group member.

Recommended for these problems

Model of human occupation	Life-style performance model

Vol.   – limited self-concept
      – loss of internal locus of control as indicated by difficulty differentiating feelings
      – difficulty initiating social interaction
      – decreased belief in self as indicated by low self-esteem
Hab. – feelings of incompetence
	Psyc. – lowered ability to assess personal skills
	      – difficulty understanding and expressing feelings
	      – loss of self-esteem
	Intp. – limited interpersonal skills

Stage of group development   This exercise is most successful when it is done with a group in which the members have developed some interest in one another.

Synopsis   All the group members give imaginary gifts to one another. These are delivered in written form.[1]

Materials and equipment   Paper
Pencils
Use a room with table and chairs.

Procedure

Invite the group members to sit around the table; then hand out a sheet of paper and pencil to each person.

---

1. This exercise can be done verbally if the group members are well motivated and able to be spontaneous. It can also be used verbally as a welcoming or farewell gesture towards a specific group member.

Give the following directions:
'Fold and tear your piece of paper so that you have the same number of pieces as there are people in the group'

This step is useful to observe anyone with particular perceptual difficulties

---

'On each slip write a name and the gift, such as a specific wish, that you would like to give to that person'
'Take time to think carefully about each person so that you can make your gifts appropriate, personal and different for each one of us'

To provide an opportunity for making a positive gesture towards other people

---

When most people have finished ask:
'Does anyone need more time?'

To give those who have not finished the responsibility of informing the group when they are finished

---

When everyone is ready ask them to give their slips of paper to the appropriate people

---

Each person is then invited to read out his collection of gifts

The gifts received not only give a measure of the impression we make on others, but also tend to be a joyful collection that enhances the self-concept

---

He is asked not to identify the person who gave him each gift

This ensures that the gift remains a personal and private gesture between two individuals

---

Discussion topics — How difficult is it to give and receive compliments?
— How each person felt about his collection of gifts.

Variations

Hand puppets

Allow 5–10 minutes per pair

This is an exercise to help a person talk easily and with more confidence in a group situation. It may also stimulate a greater awareness in him of one of the nonverbal aspects of communication, i.e. hand gestures.[1]

Recommended for these problems

Model of human occupation	Life-style performance model
Vol. – decreased belief in self as indicated by difficulty talking in a group situation	Sens/mo. – slowed sensory motor output
Hab. – feelings of incompetence	Cog. – slowness in thought-processing
Perf. – deficiencies in process skills as indicated by difficulty thinking quickly	Intp. – limited skills in verbal group interaction
– slowing of perceptual-motor skills	

Stage of group development　This exercise is most successful with a group in which the participants are fairly comfortable with each other.

Synopsis　This is a *theatre game* in which two people stand up, one behind the other, before an audience (made up of the rest of the group). The front person delivers a short speech, while the back person, placing his arms forward so that they appear to belong to his partner, uses his hands to augment what is being said.

Materials and equipment　None
Use a familiar and preferably carpeted room.

---

1. The exercise is suitable for *videotaping*. The replay will be fun to watch and will enable the participants to look carefully at such speaking skills as:
    being able to talk loudly
    being able to talk at a reasonable pace, and
    being able to talk in an interesting manner.
   The replay will show if each person was able to organize and express his thoughts clearly. It will also illustrate the importance of hand gestures and the part they play in communication.

Procedure

Invite the players to sit down on the floor in a group	This brings everyone together as a cohesive unit to form the audience
Ask if there are two volunteers of about the same height, who are willing to stand up before the audience, one (*B*) behind the other (*A*)[2]	It is important to provide an opportunity for each person to make the decision about whether he wishes to participate. Working with another person should be easier and less frightening than doing it alone
Explain the exercise as follows: '*A* holds *B* close to his own body, by clasping his hands behind *B*'s back, and . . .	Standing very close together will assist them to work more easily as one unit

'*B* puts his arms forward so that they look as though they belong to *A* (see illustration)'

'*A* then delivers a short speech to the audience . . .[3]	Encourage *A* to talk spontaneously even if it is only for a very short time
'and his partner (*B*), using his hands, gesticulates in order to augment what is being said'	To work as a team, *B* will have to concentrate on what *A* is saying

2. An alternative is to have one pair of players carrying on a conversation with another pair. As the number of people on *stage* increases so the amount of attention focused on each individual decreases. This may encourage more people to participate.
3. If *A* does not have any ideas the therapist should have a few suggestions prepared. (See Suggestions at the end of the exercise.)

Encourage the audience to participate with laughter, applause, etc.	This is very important as it provides positive support and encouragement for the two players

'Then, keeping the same positions, the procedure can be reversed, i.e. *B* gesticulates and . . . 'A makes up a monologue to fit the motions of *B*'s hands'[4]	In this way *A* is encouraged to speak impulsively, without being self-conscious

Suggestions for 'Hand puppets'

— A politician giving an election speech
— A person giving the vote of thanks after a lecture
— A demonstrator in a store, selling an all-purpose chopping utensil
— An announcer giving a weather forecast or reading the news
— Telling a story
— One person interviewing another who has just climbed the highest mountain in the world, or eaten the most hamburgers
— Two women having a conversation about some clothes they have purchased

Variations

---

4. Stress that the sentences do not have to form a logical story as long as they fit the gestures and actions. This should help to introduce an atmosphere of comedy and enjoyment into the exercise.

Happiness

Allow 1 hour

This exercise uses reminiscing to help a person feel positive about himself. This positive energy which has been generated can then be used to maintain the stamina required by the individual in order to work on his problems of the present.

Recommended for these problems

Model of human occupation	Life-style performance model
Vol. – depression as indicated by feelings of hopelessness or aimlessness – loss of sense of identity – decreased belief in self as indicated by loss of self-esteem Hab. – feelings of incompetence – loss of valued roles Perf. – impairment of interpersonal communication skills as indicated by social anxiety and isolation	Psyc. – depression – feelings of anxiety – loss of self-esteem Intp. – limited social interaction

Stage of group development This exercise can be used at any stage of group cohesion.

Synopsis In this exercise each person relaxes and recalls a pleasant experience, then reproduces that vision on paper and shares the images which he has remembered.

Materials and equipment White paper
Felt pens, crayons
Chairs around a table.

Procedure

Ask the group members, seated around a table, to assume a position that is comfortable and relaxed. Encourage them to uncross their arms, legs, or feet and let their hands lie loosely but supported. Ask them to close their eyes and take a deep breath and then let it out.

To avoid distraction from external stimuli and assist each person to become still, both physically and mentally — images will occur more easily in this state owing instructions:

time when you felt warm and __n; a time long ago or more recently when you had a sense that life was good[1], that you were in tune with the people and things around you and you felt peaceful, confident and completely happy.' (Pause)	To help each person relax completely and move into a deeper state of consciousness where positive feelings can emerge
'Remember the details of the place where you felt this way. Look around you and see the colours, the sounds, the smells . . . remember who was with you at that time.'	To help the individual sharpen the image he is experiencing
'I will stop speaking now for a few minutes so that you can recall and enjoy that place.'	Silence is essential now to allow personal recall
After a few minutes invite them to open their eyes and return to the present when they feel ready.	To help them to return to the present time without startling them
Ask them to take a sheet of paper and some colours[2] and reproduce the place they have just seen.[3]	
Explain that artistic quality is not important, and that any way they draw their time of great happiness will be just as it should be, since no one else can know what they have just seen.	To relieve the anxiety aroused by the fear of pictorial expression through art
Invite each member in turn to share his experience. Encourage the group to enjoy that experience with him through questions.	A sense of well being is derived this way, both personally and vicariously

1. This exercise makes it possible for depressed people to experience briefly a sense of well being. It may be necessary for them to search back to their childhood in order to find it.
2. If there is much anxiety over art therapy, keep these materials initially on a separate table out of sight but readily available when needed to eliminate any needless delay between the experience and the depiction of it.
3. A variation of this exercise is to show them a mandala and ask them to describe the experience by drawing one, depicting their impressions in colour and abstract form, using the circle's outer limits to contain that memory.

Close the group by explaining that at present they are experiencing a difficult time, that much effort is spent looking at problems, but it is useful to recall past happiness and past strengths to be able to 'recharge the batteries' and to derive the energy to face and solve these problems

To focus the individuals, in closing, on the positive aspects of this exercise, especially for those members who become depressed when comparing their emotional state now with the past

Variations

How do I appear?

Allow 1 hour

This is a projective technique which uses diagrams to help members verbalize how they perceive themselves and how that may differ from the image they present to others.

Recommended for these problems

Model of human occupation	Life-style performance model
Vol. – decreased motivation for behavioural change – decreased belief in self as indicated by low self-esteem – limited self-concept – decreased expectations of success Hab. – loss of identity as indicated by role imbalance Perf. – deficiency in process skills as indicated by difficulty planning	Cog. – limited motivation for behavioural change Psyc. – loss of self-esteem – lowered ability to assess personal skills

Stage of group development   Use this exercise with group members who have formed some bonds of trust and are willing to share feelings with each other.

Synopsis   Three drawings are made by each person to contrast outward appearances with personal identity and to help suggest ways of changing.

Materials and equipment   Table and chairs
Pencils with erasers
White paper.

Procedure

Hand out a sheet of paper and pencil to each person

Ask them to fold their sheet of paper into thirds. Demonstrate with your own paper

At this point the therapist can assess which members have difficulty following directions

---

1. Created by E. Storch, 1971.

Explain the exercise as follows:
'Label the first third of your paper *How others see me*, the middle third *How I see myself*, and the final third *How I would like to be seen*'

'Now draw diagrams and symbols to depict yourself in each of the three areas'	Using symbols rather than words may release feelings from below the conscious and, therefore, censorable level
When most people seem to have finished ask 'Does anyone need more time?'	To give those who are not ready the responsibility for informing the group when they are finished
When everyone has completed the exercise, ask each person to explain his set of diagrams to the group Encourage the group members to respond honestly when each person is discussing the category *How others see me*. Be prepared to help each person handle confrontation Encourage the group members to be constructive with any critical feedback they may give	This gives each person an opportunity to see if his perceptions about how others view him are correct

Discussion topics — Being misunderstood
— Appearances are deceiving
— Putting forward a favourable image
— Accuracy of self-perception

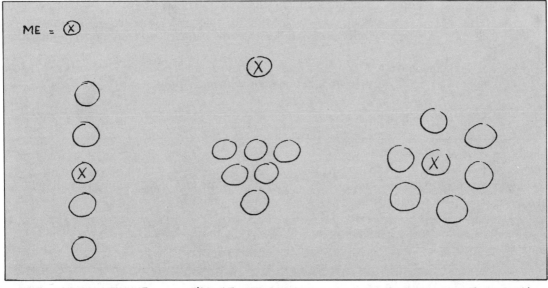

HOW OTHERS SEE ME   HOW I SEE MYSELF   HOW I WOULD LIKE TO BE SEEN

Introductions

Allow 1 hour

This exercise offers an opportunity to practise conversing with one person and then to express what one has learned to a group of people.

Recommended for these problems

Model of human occupation	Life-style performance model
Vol. – decreased belief in self as indicated by: 　　　low self-esteem 　　　hopelessness Perf. – impairment of interpersonal communication skills 　　　as indicated by: 　　　social isolation 　　　limited conversation skills	Psyc. – loss of self-esteem Intp. – limited social interaction 　　　– withdrawal from reciprocal interpersonal 　　　relationships 　　　– limited conversation skills

Stage of group development

This is an ideal exercise for a group containing several new members, or for one in which the participants are particularly isolated and withdrawn.

Synopsis

The group divides up into pairs and each pair becomes acquainted with one another through conversation. Then, each person in turn introduces and describes his partner to the remainder of the group.

Materials and equipment

A comfortable room where simultaneous conversations can be carried on without conflicting with each other.

Procedure

Explain the exercise as follows: 'In order to get to know each other better, we are each going to take turns to describe and introduce one other person to the group'	The purpose of the exercise is explained in order to allay the fear of the unknown often held by new members
'Choose a partner with whom you feel most comfortable'[1]	To eliminate some of the awkwardness in communication

1. If the group members are quite self-assured, suggest that they choose the person they know least, but whom they would like to get to know, as a partner.

'Move to a quiet spot in the room and say to your partner, "Tell me all about yourself." Collect as much information as he is willing to tell you. At the same time, he will be trying to learn all about you. In ten minutes, we will reform into a large group'

The competitive element in this exercise stimulates rapid two-way conversation and motivates interest in the other person. This time limit gives a work-oriented approach to the exercise

In ten minutes say, 'Your ten minutes are up. Please move into a large circle'

To unite physically and thereby create some cohesion in the divided group

When everyone is seated ask, 'Who would like to begin to introduce his partner by name and by description?'

To give an opportunity for an individual to be assertive
Being described by another person and hearing someone else describe oneself often reaffirms one's self-concept

Continue encouraging each person to take his turn when he feels ready to do so

When a person is introduced by someone else they tend to give details about that person that otherwise would have been withheld out of modesty

Discussion topics
— What feelings did each person experience while doing the exercise?
— Within each pair, how did the conversation go (i.e. did both participate equally, or one more than the other)?
— What social situations do you find yourself in where this type of conversation would be both appropriate and necessary?

Variations

Kim's game

Allow 30 minutes

The purpose of this exercise is to improve an individual's perception and memory, particularly in relation to objects. It takes the form of a competitive game.

Recommended for these problems

Model of human occupation	Life-style performance model

Vol. – loss of internal locus of control as indicated by lack of interaction with the environment
Perf. – decreased concentration as indicated by forgetfulness
	Cog. – short attention span
	     – diminished retention and recall
	Psyc. – apathy
	     – difficulty sustaining contact with external stimuli

Stage of group development   This is an excellent exercise to use with a group who are not physically active and have a short attention span.

Synopsis   A tray of common objects is presented for the participants to look at. After a short period of time, this tray is removed from sight. The players attempt to recall as many of the objects as they can.

Materials and equipment   Tray
Small common objects[1]
Pencils, paper
Room with table and chairs.

Procedure

Invite the participants to sit around the table and each[2] take a pencil and paper	To provide an opportunity for each person to be physically involved in the exercise

---

1. Objects that represent different aspects of life outside the hospital are useful for in-patients, as they provide contact with reality.
2. This game can be played by individuals, pairs, or teams according to the needs of the participants. For example, if they are very isolated then have them play in twos or threes since this will necessitate the interaction of one person with another and the sharing of ideas.

Explain the game as follows:
'I shall place a tray with 25[3] objects on it,
in the middle of the table'

'You will have four minutes to look at the tray and memorize the objects'	To encourage concentration, attention to detail and memorization
'The tray will then be removed and each of you will write down as many of the objects as you can recall'	To practise the skill of immediate recall
'I shall then bring back the tray for you to check your answers'	To enable each person to measure his level of achievement

Discussion topics — What methods are there to help us remember things and people's names?
— In what situations is a good memory important?

Variations

---

3. The number of objects on the tray should be varied according to the mental state of the participants. It is better to start with a low number of objects and increase the number each time the game is played, so as to provide a sense of accomplishment and improvement amongst the participants. This may in turn increase their motivation. To provide a sense of involvement and responsibility, the therapist may wish to invite some of the players to put together their own trays of objects and in turn present them to the group. This provides an opportunity for the individual to use his initiative and also may assist the therapist in her assessment of him.

Life positions (warm-up)

Allow 10–30 minutes

This is *warm-up* exercise designed to stimulate the participants by physical activity and to provide an opportunity for them to be aggressive in a nonverbal and constructive way. In the exercise the participants can also explore their role in life as related to the submissive/dominant continuum.[1]

Recommended for these problems

Model of human occupation	Life-style performance model
Vol. – decreased belief in social abilities as indicated by lack of assertiveness in interactions – difficulty differentiating feelings due to feelings of powerlessness over personal actions. Hab. – role imbalance Perf. – impairment of interpersonal communication skills as indicated by social anxiety	Psyc. – difficulty understanding and expressing feelings – feelings of anxiety Intp. – lowered ability to assess interpersonal skills

Stage of group development The exercise is appropriate for a group whose members need a constructive outlet for their energy.[2]

Synopsis The group members are divided into small teams. In each team the leader is denoted as being the most dominant and the last person as the least dominant. The team members then fight, without speaking, for the position on their team in which they feel most comfortable.

Materials and equipment None
Use a room which is carpeted and has a long vacant wall with plenty of free space in front of it.

---

1. The exercise has proven to be very stimulating and an excellent means of increasing group cohesion and verbal participation.
2. Caution should be exercised if some group members are in poor physical condition.

Procedure

Randomly select three people[3] (e.g. *A*, *B* and *C*) and ask them to stand facing the wall about two to three metres apart

Then ask the remaining group members (See '*X*' in the diagram) to line up behind *A*, *B* and *C* to form teams of approximately equal numbers

In this way each person is given the opportunity to make an initial decision, (namely, which team he/she would like to be in), and to follow through on it

```
        A   X X X X X
WALL    B   X X X X X
        C   X X X X X
```

Explain the exercise as follows:
'The position closest to the wall will be held by the most dominant person in your team. The position at the back of the team will be held by the least dominant person. Those positions in between represent degrees of dominance between the two extremes'

'Bearing this in mind, and without speaking, I would like you to fight physically for the position in your team in which you personally feel most comfortable'

To encourage physical contact and expression of feelings in a nonverbal manner

Allow the teams to fight on until each person is satisfied with the position he/she attains[4]

Then invite each team to sit down where they are[5] and discuss amongst themselves their reactions to the exercise before sharing them with the whole group.

Discussion topics — How does the physical contact affect you? Discuss:
    (a) fears,
    (b) associated feelings – positive or negative, and
    (c) how each person fought.
— What reaction does each person have to the others and the positions they finally chose?

---

3. The number chosen will depend on the number of people in the group, as each team should have at least five members.
4. Coaching by therapist — 'no sharing of positions'
                     — 'no speaking'.
5. If the number of teams is large and the therapist wishes to demonstrate the technique (e.g. to other professionals) then it is practical that one team only discusses while everyone else observes.

— What reasons did each person have for choosing his final position?
— How does each person's behaviour during the game relate to his daily life? Is this how he deals with friends, family situations, work, etc.? Is it appropriate and satisfactory? Is it how he likes to be? Does he achieve his goals?

Variations

Likes and dislikes

Allow 1 hour

This is an exercise in self-awareness and communication.

Recommended for these problems

Model of human occupation	Life-style performance model

Vol. – inability to make decisions
    – decreased belief in self as indicated by difficulty talking in a group situation
    – limited self-concept
    – diminished sense of personal effectiveness
    – difficulty describing interests
Perf. – impairment of interpersonal communication skills as indicated by social isolation
	Psyc. – ambivalence
	    – lowered ability to assess personal skills
	    – loss of self-reliance
	Intp. – limited skills in verbal group interaction
	    – limited social interaction

Stage of group development This is an exercise which enables an unfamiliar, incohesive group to get to know one another and begin to interact.

Synopsis It requires that each person list the five things they like most and the five things they dislike most on opposite sides of a piece of paper. This information is then used as a basis for discussion.

Materials and equipment
Sheets of paper
Pencils
Erasers
Room with a table and chairs.

Procedure

Invite the group members to sit around the table	To promote a sense of security and purpose (the solid table ensures a definite distance between the people)
Ask them to pass around the pencils and paper, keeping one each for themselves	To encourage a decision on the part of each person to participate actively

give the following instructions:
| one side of your piece of paper with the
word *Likes*. Then turn it over and label the other
side with the word *Dislikes'*

'Under the appropriate heading write the five things you like most and the five you dislike most'[1]	To encourage self-awareness through the process of evaluation and discrimination. The lists compiled are usually factual and relate to recent events in each person's life
'You have ten minutes in which to do this'	To provide a time limit within which to work and encourage each person to apply himself to the task
After this time the sheets of paper will be redistributed amongst the group so that no one has his own[2]	This allows the shy person to describe himself through someone else
'Each person will have an opportunity to read out what is written on the sheet of paper he holds, so that the group can try to guess who wrote it and discuss the contents'[3]	To promote increased awareness of each other as interesting and unique individuals To encourage verbal expression and interaction The puzzle elements make the exercise more stimulating

Variations

1. There are many possible variations. The following are just a few examples: *Things you like doing, things you dislike doing* (to assist awareness of how the person spends his time), *Ways in which you behave towards other people, which they like or dislike* (to aid self-awareness and evaluation of the effect of one's behaviour upon others), *Identify problems that you have and list possible ways of dealing with them* (to encourage objectivity and realistic constructive thought). Role play some of the alternatives to provide an opportunity for the person to experience and/or practise some of his ideas, as well as receive feedback on the solutions.
2. The lists could be put in a hat and each person asked to choose one as he take his turn. This variation is useful when there are distractable anxious people in the group who would be reading the list given them rather than listening to the discussion.
3. Where problems, feelings or aspects of behaviour are being identified, it is important that the discussion include constructive alternatives, contributed either by the group members, the therapist or, more usefully, by the individual himself.

Allow 15–30 minutes # Magic box

This is an exercise utilizing nonverbal communication. It may assist an individual to improve his concentration and memory.[1]

Recommended for these problems

Model of human occupation	Life-style performance model
Vol. – inhibited self-expression due to decreased expectations of success – inability to make decisions Perf. – decreased concentration as indicated by forgetfulness – slowing of perceptual-motor skills	Sens/mo. – difficulty processing sensory information Cog. – difficulty making choices – short attention span – diminished retention and recall – inhibited self-expression

Stage of group development

This exercise is best used with a small group of people; they need not be familiar with one another.

Synopsis

This is a progressive game that makes use of an imaginary box. Each player, in turn, receives the *box* and, on opening it, has to take out and use all the previously created *objects* that it contains. He then adds one of his own, closes the lid, and passes the box on.

This exercise could be used in conjunction with other memory exercises such as *Kim's game* or *Find the change*.

Materials and equipment

None
Use a familiar room that is carpeted.

Procedure

Invite the group members to sit on the floor in a circle of less than ten[2] people	To form a small unit of people who will feel at ease working together

1. This exercise is suitable for *videotaping*. The replay will be fun to watch and will allow each person to see his ability to be creative and uninhibited.
2. The amount of information that each person has to memorise is directly proportionate to the number of people in the group. If the attention span of the participants is short, it is advisable that the group be divided into smaller units.

Designate a leader in each group[3]

Explain the exercise as follows: 'The leader will mime an imaginary *box* (its shape, size, weight, and texture, etc.) which he will produce and place on the floor in front of him'	To provide an opportunity for creative self-expression
'He will open it and invent a mime *object* which he will use in such a way that its identity is obvious to the rest of us'	To encourage contact with reality by recalling the use of familiar objects and to practise communication
'Then he will place the object in the *box*, close the lid, and pass it on to the next person'[4]	To enable each person in the group to participate
'This player will open the *box*, remove the imagined object and use it in the same or a different manner . . .	This part of the exercise requires memory, imagination and concentration
'then, placing it back in the *box*, he will invent his own mime *object* which he will use and place in the *box* too'	
'Closing the lid he will pass the *box* on to the next player'[5]	To encourage interaction between the two people
The *box* continues around the circle with each person using all of the previously invented *objects* and then adding one of his own	As the game progresses, there is an increasing amount of concentration, memory and initiative required on the part of each successive person
When the *box* finally returns to the leader, he removes all the *objects* one by one, uses them and then throws them away	To conclude the game symbolically

Variations

---

3. If the exercise is familiar invite volunteers to take the position of leader in the group.
4. If the players are at all confused, specify the direction in which they pass the *box* (e.g. 'Pass the *box* to the person on your right.').
5. The therapist (leader) may need to remind the participants to remember the size, shape and weight of the *box*, as well as the contents.

Allow 1 hour # Masks

This is an exercise in self-awareness which focuses on how people use their facial expression as a means of defence.[1]

Recommended for these problems

Model of human occupation	Life-style performance model

Vol. – loss of internal locus of control as indicated by:
    lack of insight
    difficulty differentiating and expressing feelings
Perf. – decreased social involvement
	Psyc. – difficulty understanding and expressing feelings
	    – lowered ability to assess personal skills
	Intp. – withdrawal from reciprocal interpersonal
	    relationships

Stage of group development This exercise is suitable to use with a group that has worked together for a few sessions and whose members are beginning to trust one another.

Synopsis Each person is asked to draw his own face twice, firstly in terms of how others see it, and secondly in terms of how he actually feels inside. The group then discuss the resulting pictures.

Materials and equipment Sheets of moderately stiff paper, about 20 cm × 28 cm
Felt pens (wide colour range)
Pencils
Room with table and chairs.

Procedure

Invite the group members to sit around the table . . .	To promote a sense of group cohesion and a purposeful atmosphere
and each to take two sheets of paper	This encourages each person to make the decision whether he will participate in the exercise or not

1. Created by E. Storch, 1973.

Place the felt pens in the centre of the table	To encourage cooperative interaction while working
Give the following instructions: 'On one of your pieces of paper draw a picture of your face which shows how you think it appears to other people. Title this *How I appear to others'*	To assist each person to be objective with regard to his outward appearance
When everyone has finished, continue with the second part of the exercise	
'Now, thinking carefully of how you feel inside, draw another picture of your face (using the second piece of paper) to show how you actually feel. Title this *How I actually feel'*	To increase the awareness of feelings at a particular point in time and to assist differentiation between outward and inward expression of them To aid the therapist's assessment of each person's mental state
When everyone has finished both parts of the exercise, invite each person to show the group his two drawings and to explain them	To provide each person with an opportunity to explain his own drawings and promote increased awareness amongst everyone of how facial expression can be used to mask real feelings

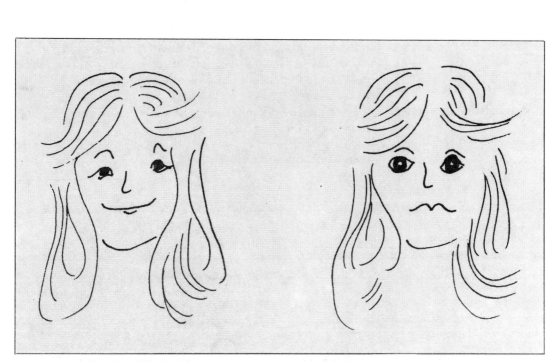

HOW I APPEAR   HOW I ACTUALLY FEEL

Encourage the group members to discuss any
ideas or reactions they may have

Also invite them to become more aware of how often they notice themselves and others using their *mask* rather than expressing their real feelings	This may promote greater self-awareness and encourage the giving and receiving of personal comments

Note: Displaying the *masks* on the walls of the
group's room can act as a reminder to them of
the exercise

Discussion topics   — What are the reasons for masking one's feelings?
— What are the effects upon oneself and others of masking one's feelings?
— How does each person's self-image compare with how other people see him?

Variations

Allow 5–15 minutes # Mirrors

This is an exercise to help a person improve his ability to communicate and interact with another person.[1]

Recommended for these problems

Model of human occupation	Life-style performance model

Vol.   – impairment of interpersonal communication as indicated by:
     decreased eye contact
     social isolation
  – distorted body image
  – inhibited self-expression due to decreased expectations of success
Perf. – decreased concentration (5–15 minutes)
	Sens/mo. – distorted body image
	Cog. – short attention span
	Psyc. – inhibited self-expression
	Intp. – fear of eye contact
	      – limited social interaction

Stage of group development   This is an appropriate exercise to use when there is little interaction between group members.

Synopsis   Two people stand facing one another. First they make eye-contact and try to maintain it throughout the remainder of the exercise. Then, one of them (*the leader*) moves a part or parts of his body very slowly and his partner (*the follower*) tries to mirror the motion exactly. The pair switch roles several times and then they attempt to continue moving and reflecting each other's moves with neither one of them consciously leading.

Materials and equipment   None required[2]
Use a familiar room that is quiet.

---

1. The exercise is suitable for *videotaping*. The replay will enable the participants to see how they reacted during the exercise. They will be able to view their emotional and physical responses in the two different roles.
2. This exercise could be done using music as a means of suggesting patterns of movement to the participants. There is a list of pieces of music that could be used immediately following the exercise *Painting to music*, p. 101.

Procedure

Invite the group members to divide into pairs, choosing a partner whom they feel at ease with, and with whom they would like to work	This is to encourage each person to become aware of the other group members and to contact one of them in particular
Explain the exercise as follows: 'Stand about one metre away from your partner and look him firmly in the eye'	For those people who find making and maintaining eye-contact very difficult it is important that they have a chance to practise. If everyone does the exercise simultaneously it will help those who are at all self-conscious
'When you both feel comfortable, decide between you who will be the *leader* and who will be the *follower*'	This requires cooperation and decision-making between the two people
'Then, looking each other in the eye as continuously as possible, . . .	Maintaining eye-contact requires considerable concentration
'I would like the *leader* to start moving his body or a part of it *very, very* slowly' (Stress the last part)	This provides an opportunity for a person to lead and initiate actions, in a controlled and deliberate way

'At the same time as you do this your partner will try to mirror your action exactly'	This requires concentration and will exercise the *follower's* ability to perceive and mime body movements initiated by his partner
Allow each pair to practise, giving assistance or demonstration where it is necessary	To encourage everyone to become involved in the doing of the exercise and to assist them in carrying out the instructions correctly
Then invite the pairs to switch roles, so that the former *leader* becomes the *follower* and vice versa	This enables everyone to experience both roles, and may encourage versatility
When each pair has switched roles several times, continue by giving the following instructions: 'Now I would like you to move in free form: that is, with neither one of you consciously leading or following and yet each of you continuing to mirror the movements of the other'	This encourages sensitivity to another person and the experience of working simultaneously with him; it also requires greater concentration
When the exercise is over, ask the group members to sit in a circle	
Invite them to discuss any feelings or reactions they may have experienced	To encourage the sharing of feelings evoked by an experience common to all and particularly related to the difference between being the *leader* and *follower*

Discussion topics — How did it feel to make eye-contact with another person?
— Was it easy or difficult to maintain eye-contact?
— Discuss the importance of looking at people in order to communicate more effectively.

Variations

Allow 15–30 minutes

Movement and sound circle (warm-up)

This is an exercise in self-expression, communication, and interaction. It can be used as a *warm-up*.[1]

Recommended for these problems

Model of human occupation	Life-style performance model
Vol. – inhibited self expression due to decreased expectations of success – lost of awareness of body movements Perf. – slowing of perceptual-motor skills	Sens/mo. – slowed sensory motor output – decreased body awareness Psyc. – inhibited self-expression

Stage of group development   This is an appropriate exercise for a group in which the members find communication difficult.

Synopsis   This exercise takes the form of a game where one player, standing in the centre of a circle, initiates a repetitive movement and an associated sound (e.g. marching to the sound 'boom, boom, boom'). He then teaches his movement and sound to another player who attempts to imitate both of them as closely as possible. The two people exchange positions and the new player develops the learned *movement and sound* into a different *movement and sound* of his own making.

Materials and equipment   None
Use a familiar room that is quiet.

Procedure

Invite the group members to stand in a circle	This enables each person to see and, therefore, be more aware of everyone else

---

1. The exercise is suitable for *videotaping*. The replay can be watched just for fun and will allow participants to see themselves creating uninhibited body movements and associated sounds.

Explain the exercise as follows: 'One person stands in the centre of the circle[2,3] and . . .	To provide a focus for the attention of the group members
'initiates a repetitive movement, and in conjunction with it — a fitting sound'[4,5,6]	To provide an opportunity for self-expression in the form of repetitive physical activity and simple verbalization
'When the movement and sound have evolved to his satisfaction[7] . . .	
'he moves to stand in front of one of the players in the surrounding circle'	To encourage awareness of others and provide an opportunity to make a choice from a selection of alternatives
'He teaches his movement and sound to this person'[8]	To encourage communication
'The player being taught tries to imitate both the action and the sound as closely as he can'[9]	To encourage interaction while concentrating upon another person To assist self-awareness, since both the individuals are receiving visual feedback on how their actions appear
'When the *teacher* is satisfied that his movement and sound have been learned accurately, the two players change positions	

2. If the game is being played for the first time, the therapist is advised to take this position in order to demonstrate the instructions he gives. If, however, the players are familiar with the exercise, ask if there is a volunteer who would like to be in the centre of the circle. This provides an opportunity for someone to demonstrate initiative.
3. If the players are hesitant to be the only person in the centre, because it means they are the focus of everyone's attention, it may be advisable to begin with two or even three people there. Each one of them teaches his own 'movement and sound' simultaneously.
4. With some groups (e.g. those who find it difficult to cope with more than one idea at a time), simplify the exercise. Begin with the movements and include the sounds as the group members become relaxed.
5. Encourage the players to keep the actions large and the sounds simple and loud, since they are easier to imitate and tend to be more stimulating.
6. As the players become more proficient, they may be encouraged to introduce words and phrases instead of simple sounds. A question and answer situation may develop or even a continuing story.
7. Ideally the movement and sound should evolve naturally to suit the person in the centre of the circle. Therefore, the therapist must discourage him from stopping to think, fumble or wonder 'What shall I do?'.
8. If the whole group imitates the action and sound as it is being taught this will encourage both an enthusiastic and energetic response. It may also help to keep the energy level up during the evolution of new action and sounds and tend to give the central player encouragement and support.
9. Encourage the action and sound to be repeated over and over again until the player can imitate them to the best of his ability.

'The new player takes his learned movement and sound into the centre of the circle where he allows them to develop[10] into a different movement and sound of his own making'

He then teaches his own movement and sound to another player and so the exercise progresses	To enable everyone to take part in the exercise. The random choice of who goes into the centre of the circle tends to increase the spontaneity and is less anxiety-provoking than waiting to go in a particular order
After the exercise is over you may like to invite the group members to discuss their reactions briefly. This exercise is often used as a *warm-up*, in which case discussion may be more appropriate at the end of the session	To encourage expression of feelings evoked by the exercise

Variations

---

10.   Develop, that is, by exaggerating or distorting the sound and movement.

Mystery objects

Allow 10–30 minutes

This is an exercise in tactile perception.

Recommended for these problems

Model of human occupation	Life-style performance model
Vol. – decreased belief in self as indicated by loss of self-esteem and difficulty talking in a group situation Perf. – difficulty interpreting sensory cues	Sens/mo. – decreased visual/tactile discrimination Psyc. – loss of self-esteem – difficulty sustaining contact with external stimuli Intp. – limited interpersonal skills

Stage of group development This exercise is useful for a group whose members have difficulty talking to one another.

Synopsis It takes the form of a *theatre game* in which a player is given a small article to hold behind his back. Then, using his sense of touch, he tries to answer questions about the article, and guess its identity.

Materials and equipment Container
50 small articles.

Procedure

Beforehand invite all the players to bring a number of small articles, collected from home[1] to the activity	To encourage a sense of responsibility and involvement in the group's activities
Prior to beginning the game, pass the container around for each person to place his contributions in, without revealing them to the others.	

---

1. In-patients can be invited to bring articles from within the hospital setting, or personal belongings.

Then invite the players to sit down in a circle and ask if there is a *volunteer* willing to stand up in front of everybody	To provide an opportunity for a group member to take a risk in a warm supportive environment
Explain the exercise as follows: 'The *volunteer* stands with his back to the group and his hands behind him'	
'The *leader*[2] takes an object out of the bag and places it in the hands of the *volunteer*'	
'He then asks the *volunteer* six or seven questions about the article[3] (e.g. "What shape is it?" "What size is it?" "How does it feel?" and amusing questions, such as "What colour do you think it is?" and finally "Do you know what the article is?")'	To provide the *volunteer* with an opportunity to arrive at a decision using tactile discrimination and deduction
'The *volunteer* attempts to answer these to the best of his ability, without looking.' (As the group can see the article some of the questions and answers can be very amusing)	To improve tactile perception and verbal interaction related to an everyday object
After a given number of questions (e.g. 10), the *volunteer* is invited to look at the object before placing it back in the bag. He then returns to his place in the circle	So that he can compare his visual perception with what he sensed by touch
Encourage the audience to applaud and then . . .	To provide the group member with a rewarding and supportive conclusion to his turn
invite another *volunteer* to come forward.[4]	

2. Once the therapist has demonstrated how the game is played, the position of *leader* can be taken by a group member.
3. Encourage seated group members to think of questions to ask as this will help them to feel more involved.
4. This exercise can be adapted for patients who are very withdrawn and isolated. If simple, everyday objects are used, the chances of success in identification are considerably increased.

Name game (warm-up)

Allow 30 minutes

This *warm-up* technique helps new members learn the names of other people in the group and provides each person with an opportunity to share something about himself. It also exercises concentration and memory.[1]

Recommended for these problems

Model of human occupation	Life-style performance model
Vol. – difficulty initiating conversation Hab. – loss of valued roles Perf. – decreased concentration as indicated by forgetfulness	Cog. – short attention span – diminished retention and recall Intp. – limited ability to initiate conversation

Stage of group development It is a good exercise to use when working with a group which contains several new members.

Synopsis This is a progressive *theatre game* in which each person introduces himself by name to the group and then shares something personal. Having done this he then tries to remember the names and personal contributions of all the people preceding him. If he cannot do this, the game begins again.

Materials and equipment None
Use a room large enough for everyone to sit in a circle and be comfortable.

Procedure

Invite the group members to sit in a circle

---

1. The exercise is suitable for *videotaping*. Watching the replay will provide each person with an opportunity to look at himself and his own behaviour more objectively. Specifically, the tape will show any habits participants have which make communication difficult or impossible (e.g. avoiding eye-contact, mumbling, speaking very softly, not paying attention, etc.). Once the habits have been identified each person is in a position to start learning more appropriate and effective ones.

Explain the exercise as follows:

'We are going to start today with a *theatre game* to help improve our concentration and memory. It will give us a chance to practise the art of introducing ourselves to another person and will help the new members learn our names'	An explanation of the purpose of the exercise may help to allay any anxiety the participants feel
'One person begins by introducing himself to the person on his left, saying, "Hi, my name is *X*." He then tells that person something about himself'[2]	This encourages a person to make specific contact with another person. This gives an opportunity for the group to begin learning something about each other's lives
'The person he is addressing then repeats what he has heard from *X*, and turning to the person on *his* left, introduces himself and gives a personal fact. And so it continues around the circle until the last person, who must recite all the names and facts, tells them to *X*'	
'If at any time one of us cannot remember either a name or fact correctly then the game will start again at the beginning[3] The game is finished when everyone has had his turn'	This is so that the person who has difficulty remembering has another opportunity to learn the names
To start this exercise the therapist may either ask for a *volunteer* or designate someone, bearing in mind that since the game is a progressive one the last person to play has to remember considerably more than the first[4]	

Discussion topics[5]
— What does it feel like to be in a room full of strangers?
— Why is it important to remember a person's name?
— Discuss the importance of being able to share personal facts when talking to another person.
— Discuss the importance of paying attention to a person's replies if one is interested in continuing the conversation.

Variations

2. Initially invite group members to share superficial facts about themselves, such as 'What is their favourite kind of food?' or 'What do they like doing most in their spare time?'. If the group members know one another well then this exercise is an excellent way to help them start sharing facts of a more personal and insightful nature, such as 'What problem brings you to this group?'
3. Go back to the person who started and play the game exactly as before with each person sharing the same personal fact.
4. Cf. *Magic box*, p. 79.
5. Since this game is primarily a *warm-up* technique it is likely that discussion will not follow it immediately, but after other exercises have been used.

Allow 1 hour Newspaper quiz

This is a technique to stimulate interest in and awareness of current events. It also encourages teamwork.

Recommended for these problems

Model of human occupation	Life-style performance model
Vol. – decreased belief in self as indicated by difficulty talking in a group situation – limited awareness of community resources – loss of internal locus of control as indicated by lack of interaction with the environment Perf. – inability to problem solve	Cog. – difficulty problem solving – limited skills in community awareness Psyc. – difficulty sustaining contact with external stimuli Intp. – limited skills in verbal group interaction

Stage of group development This exercise can be used with a variety of groups but, because of its competitive element, it is particularly useful in fostering group cohesion.

Synopsis The exercise takes the form of a competitive game in which each team has to hunt through a newspaper for the answer to a specific question.

Materials and equipment 1 complete daily newspaper for each team of 3 to 4 people
1 table for each team
Chairs
Paper
Pencils
Blackboard and chalk upon which a visual record of the results can be kept.

Procedure

Beforehand prepare a list of questions,[1] the answers to which will be found in the newspaper. Number or label the tables.

Invite the group members to form teams of three or four people and sit one team to a table	To form a team requires making contact with other people

---

Give the following instructions:
'On your table you will find a number which represents your team, a complete copy of today's newspaper and some pencils and paper'

Ask if there are volunteers willing to be the *question-master* or *score-keeper*. The therapist may need to assist the volunteers	Being *question-master* or *score-keeper* can be a suitable role for someone who feels the exercise is beneath him or for someone who might otherwise remain uninvolved

---

'The *question-master* will read out a question and . . .	This requires clear, distinct speech

---

'the first team to find the correct answer in the newspaper will receive a point'[2]	To encourage a sense of competition and cooperative interaction between the members of each team. At this time the therapist can observe how each person participates within his team

---

'The score-keeper will assign a point to the appropriate team and then the *question-master* will go on to the next question'	To provide an opportunity for responsibility and cooperation between the teams and the volunteers

---

'The winning team will be the one which obtains the highest number of points overall'[3]	To provide an incentive for maximum effort and participation

---

1. In preparing the questions consider these points:
   Should you choose information in large print if there are some group members who are on large amounts of medication and have blurred vision?
   Are the questions difficult enough to be stimulating, yet easy enough to provide a sense of achievement?
   Do you need to give hints on the location of the answer in the paper?
   Have you prepared enough questions? (Allow approximately one minute per question.)
   Could the members' knowledge of current events be expanded?
2. When there are more than two teams competing, it may be advisable that they write their answers down rather than call them out. The answers can be checked at the end of the quiz.
3. With some patients (e.g. children, adolescents, or chronically disabled adults), a prize for the winning team may be the additional stimulus which helps to maintain their interest and involvement.

Suggestions for
'Newspaper quiz' questions

— What is today's weather forecast?
— What film is now playing at the *Odeon*?
— Who won the football game last night?
— What store is advertising a Winter Sale?
— Which large building was reported to have burned down last night?
— What problem was Mr Brown writing about in *Letters to the Editor*?
— At what times can you watch a television news bulletin during the evening?
— What is today's horoscope for those born in the beginning of May?
— On what page are *Jobs Available* advertised?
— How much rent is being asked for the one bedroom apartment at 1611 Forge Street?

Variations

Nicknames (warm-up)

Allow 20 minutes

This is a *warm-up* exercise. It stimulates group members to be physically active and helps them get to know each other better.[1]

Recommended for these problems

Model of human occupation	Life-style performance model
Vol. – loss of sense of identity Perf. – decreased social involvement resulting in social isolation – difficulty initiating social interaction – slowing of perceptual-motor skills	Sens/mo. – slowed sensory/motor output Intp. – limited social interaction – limited ability to initiate conversation

Stage of group development

This is an excellent exercise to use with a group of people who do not know one another.

Synopsis

Each person identifies himself on a name tag. The object of the game is to be the first person to record on paper everyone else's name.

Materials and equipment

A spacious room
Pencils
Name tags
Pins
Sheets of paper.

Procedure

Explain the exercise as follows:
'Write on your name tag your nickname or a name that describes you'

---

1. Created by E. Storch 1973.

'Pin the tag to the back of your sleeve
When I say "start," move around, read and write
down all the names you can see'

With the name tag in this position the person has
to move about in order to avoid being identified.
This encourages (1) an increased awareness of his
position in relation to those around him and
(2) defensive tactics as he attempts to trick others
into revealing their identity

'The first person to collect all the names (the
number in the group) is the winner'

When three or more people have completed
their lists, reform as a group and ask each
person to identify himself

To satisfy the curiosity of those who had not
finished and give an opportunity for jovial
feedback between individuals

Encourage discussion about how each person
acquired his nickname

Variations

"PIN THE TAG
TO THE BACK OF
YOUR SLEEVE"

Now and the future

Allow 1 hour

This is an exercise which assists individuals to gain a deeper understanding of themselves and of each other.[1]

Recommended for these problems

Model of human occupation	**Life-style performance model**

Vol. – difficulty conceptualising future events
     – decreased expectations of success
     – loss of internal locus of control as indicated by lack
       of insight
Hab. – decreased motivation for behavioural change
     – role loss as indicated by lack of identity
Perf. – deficiency in process skills affecting planning
	Cog. – difficulty making choices
	     – limited motivation for behavioural change
	Psyc. – lowered ability to assess personal skills

Stage of group development   This exercise is best for a group that has developed some unity and in which the members have some interest in each other.

Synopsis   Each person compares his present situation with his desired future situation, depicting both of them in diagrammatic form.

Materials and equipment   White paper
Pencils and erasers
Felt pens
Table and chairs

Procedure

Invite everyone to sit around the table and help themselves to paper and pencils

Ask the group members to fold their paper in half (demonstrate with your own paper)

---

1. Created by E. Storch, 1971.

Give the following instructions:
'On the left side of your piece of paper draw *how you are now*. That is, how you are feeling and what your present life situation is. Then, on the right side, draw *how you wish to be in the future*. Draw diagrams and symbols to explain your situation. Don't be artistic or draw a self-portrait'

To give the individual an opportunity to look at his present situation clearly and to project himself into a future relieved of his present problems

When most people are finished ask 'Does anyone need more time?'

To allow those people who either have much to say or who find the exercise difficult, to work at their own speed. They will take the responsibility for telling the group when they are ready

When the group is ready, ask who would like to begin by explaining his drawings. If the discussion is awkward ask him to compare the two drawings and explain how he hopes to attain his desired future

To stimulate some dynamic thoughts about life as he sees it and possible changes he can make

Discussion topics — Discuss methods of changing present situations.
— Discuss fear of the future (e.g. jobs and other commitments).
— What it is like to feel helpless about making decisions for your life.
— Discuss taking on responsibility for one's own life and its direction.

Variations

HOW I AM NOW   HOW I WISH TO BE IN THE FUTURE

Allow 1 hour Painting to music

This is a projective exercise to assist self-expression.

Recommended for these problems

Model of human occupation	Life-style performance model

Vol. – limited self-concept
     – loss of internal locus of control as indicated by
       difficulty differentiating feelings
Perf. – difficulty expressing ideas due to limited
       interpersonal communication skills
	Cog. – difficulty expressing ideas
	Psyc. – lowered ability to assess personal skills
	       – difficulty understanding and expressing feelings

Stage of group development This exercise works well with a group of people who are acquainted with each other but need some means of expressing themselves in a group setting.

Synopsis The group listens to a short piece of music several times. Each person then creates a painting to express the images or feelings that were evoked by the music. Afterwards everyone is invited to share his experience with the other group members.

Materials and equipment Records or taped music[1]
Record player or tape deck
Sheets of paper, at least 40 cm × 50 cm
Water colour paints
Paint brushes of assorted sizes
Water containers
Newspaper
Overalls (optional)
Tables and chairs (optional)
Use a room with enough working space to promote a relaxed atmosphere.

---

1. For Suggestions refer to the end of the exercise.

Procedure

Invite everyone to sit in a circle, finding a really comfortable position	To assist each person to listen attentively to the music
Explain the exercise as follows: 'I am going to play a short extract of music through twice'[2]	Clear, concise instructions tend to reassure those who are fearful of new experiences
'As you listen to it, try to be aware of what it makes you think of and how it makes you feel'	To encourage self-awareness and concentration
'Then collect some paint and paint brushes and express these feelings on paper'	
'No doubt, we shall all experience the music differently; some of us may respond to the rhythm, others to the feelings or images aroused within ourselves'[3]	To give reassurance and encourage each person to feel safe enough to express his reactions, even if they are different from that of the person next to him The therapist should observe how each person reacts
'Wait until you feel ready to start'	To enable reluctant participants to join in later on[4]
'Later there will be an opportunity for each person to explain his painting if he so wishes'[5]	This will provide an opportunity for each person to share his reactions with the others
Encourage discussion by sharing one's own reactions and assisting group members to share theirs	To increase awareness of one's self and others, and to encourage the giving and receiving of comments

2. It is not necessary to identify the music until the end of the exercise. This should encourage the expression of spontaneous rather than preconceived ideas and feelings.
3. Patients whose ego-boundaries are diffuse have difficulty discriminating between what is real and what is unreal and may, therefore, find this exercise rather anxiety-provoking. To help overcome this, the therapist is advised to use very descriptive music (see list of Suggestions) and to concentrate initially on the images rather than on the feelings aroused. She should also give assistance and encouragement to anyone requiring it.
4. With some groups it may be advisable to set a time limit. Do not be too concerned if someone does not wish to participate — it is likely he/she will when he/she sees the others involved and at ease.
5. Our experience with this exercise has shown that:
   (a) it tends to provide the very quiet person with an opportunity to express himself.
   (b) the underlying feelings evoked in people are often similar, although their symbolic portrayal of the feelings may be different.
   (c) the most withdrawn people are often the most perceptive.

Suggestions for 'Painting to music'

(a) Musical selections suitable for stimulating a variety of emotional responses

Air on a G String	Bach
Night on the Bare Mountain	Mussorgsky
Ave Maria	Schubert
Ecossaises	Beethoven
Latin American Symphonette	Morton Gould
Moonlight Sonata: (First movement)	Beethoven
Peer Gynt Suite No. 1: (Hall of the Mountain King)	Grieg
Peer Gynt Suite No. 1: (The Death of Ase)	Grieg
Piano Concerto No. 4 in G Major (First movement Bars 1–29)	Beethoven
Rite of Spring (Part I 'Adoration of the Earth')	Stravinsky
Scheherezade Suite: (First movement)	Rimsky-Korsakov
Scherzo No. 1 in B Minor, Opus 20	Chopin
Slavonic Dance No. 2	Dvorak
Symphony No. 5 in C Minor: (First movement)	Beethoven
The Sorcerer's Apprentice	Dukas
William Tell Overture: (Finale)	Rossini
Violin Concerto in D Major: (Second movement bars 1–20)	Mozart
Xerxes (Largo)	Handel

(b) *Musical selections suitable for stimulating the imagination*

Night on the Bare Mountain	Mussorgsky
Dance of the Hours	Ponchielli
Finlandia, Opus 26	Sibelius
Nutcracker Suite	Tchaikovsky
Peer Gynt Suite	Grieg
Pictures at an Exhibition	Mussorgsky
Romeo and Juliet Overture	Tchaikovsky
Symphony No. 6 in F Major ('Pastoral'), Opus 68	Beethoven
The Planets, Opus 32	Gustav Holst
The Seasons	Glazunov
The Vltava (Moldau)	Smetana

Variations

Allow 5-10 minutes or 1 hour

Pass the ball (warm-up)

This is primarily a *warm-up* technique to provide personal introductions and assist name-learning. However, it can be extended to form an exercise in direct communication between participants[1]

Recommended for these problems

Model of human occupation	Life-style performance model
Perf. – slowing of perceptual-motor skills – difficulty initiating social interaction – decreased social involvement – impairment of interpersonal skills	Sens/mo. – slowed sensory-motor output Intp. – withdrawal from reciprocal interpersonal relationships – limited social interaction – limited ability to initiate conversation

Stage of group development This is an excellent exercise to use as a *warm-up* for a group of people who are particularly quiet or withdrawn and do not know one another.

Synopsis One person in the group passes the ball to another person and at the same time offers some verbal information about himself to the recipient.

Materials and equipment Chairs (if the participants are unable to sit on the floor)
A ball (choose a large, light one if possible).

---

1. This exercise is suitable for *videotaping*. The replay can be used to show participants how they converse with one another and, more specifically, to identify potential communication problems (e.g. avoiding eye-contact, talking very softly, answering questions in a vague or indirect way, reluctance to share personal information, etc.). If problems are identified, these can form the basis for a discussion.

Procedure

Invite the group members to sit down in as small a circle as possible[2,3]	This tends to provide physical closeness between group members and makes passing the ball across the circle easier
Place the ball in the centre of the circle and explain the exercise as follows: 'One person in the group will pick up the ball and give it to another person saying: "My name is . . ." The recipient, in turn, will give the ball to a third person saying: "My name is . . ." and so on'	This involves the simultaneous actions of making physical contact with a chosen person and introducing oneself to him. Eye-contact and clear diction are encouraged
'If, at any time, you do not wish to participate, then place the ball back in the centre of the circle'	This provides an opportunity for opting out and the decision to do so is expressed nonverbally
'Anyone else may pick up the ball and continue with the exercise'	
'When everyone has said their names several times, the sentence will be extended to include the recipient's name, i.e. "My name is . . ., your name is . . .", each time you pass the ball on'	This improves the skills of recognition and recall. The associated physical contact acts as an added stimulus for those whose attention span and/or contact with reality is poor
'Now that you have learned everyone's name, when you pass the ball on, tell the recipient something about yourself, prefixing your statement with his name'[4]	This encourages the participants to share information about themselves
The exercise can be progressed stage by stage to include such topics as 'Now tell the recipient how you are feeling today'[5,6]	This encourages the identification and expression of feelings in a direct and specific manner

2. To provide an outlet for restlessness, make the circle larger. Then ask the participants to walk across the circle and give the ball to the person they have chosen.
3. To stimulate the motor senses (e.g. reflexes, muscle coordination and control), rather than intimate interpersonal contact, increase the size of the circle. Then ask the participants to stand up and either throw or bounce the ball to one another when they speak.
4. By sharing information in this way, new members joining a group are provided with some cues for further conversation.
5. In a smaller group members will get to know and trust one another more quickly than in a larger group.
6. As therapist you can decide what information will be helpful for the players to share with one another. Suggestions can also be elicited from the group members themselves.

The exercise could be concluded in the
following manner:
'Finally, you can ask the recipient of your ball a
question. He may answer you and then he can
turn to another person with a question'

This promotes conversational exchanges between
people but in a very structured way. It encourages
the use of initiative and an awareness of other
people

Discussion topics   — Why is it important to be able to share information about our-
selves with other people?
— Why is it sometimes difficult to talk directly to another person?
— How do we avoid talking to people?

Variations

Allow 5–10 minutes # People machine

This is an exercise to encourage physical closeness in an enjoyable way. It can be used as a *warm-up* or a longer activity.

Recommended for these problems

Model of human occupation	Life-style performance model

Vol. – impairment of interpersonal communication as indicated by:
    difficulty trusting people
    social isolation
Perf. – slowing of perceptual-motor skills
    – impairment of interpersonal communication skills as indicated by:
        fear of touching people
	Sens/mo. – slowed sensory motor output
	Intp. – limited capacity for trust
	    – limited social interaction
	    – fear of physical contact

Stage of group development   This is a good exercise to use with a group who are getting to know one another.

Synopsis   It takes the form of a game where the group members join together to make a piece of moving machinery with as many moving gears and levers as they can think of.

Materials and equipment   None. A comfortable, carpeted room would be appropriate.

Procedure

Invite everyone to stand in a circle	To bring the group together
Explain the exercise as follows: 'We are going to make a piece of moving machinery'	To give an overall picture of the activity
'One of us will begin by standing in the centre of the circle'	To provide an opportunity for someone to assume leadership
'This person will think of a movement and sound that represents a small part of a large machine'	

'When he is ready he will make this movement and sound repetitively'	This allows the person to express ideas in a physical manner
'Watch him closely to get a clear idea of what he is doing'	To re-focus the attention of group members
'Then think of a movement and sound of your own'	Some people may need encouragement at this time
'When you are ready, move in to the centre of the circle, and . . .	To encourage personal decision-making
'attach yourself in some way to another person'	It is important that the participants link up with one another physically
'Then begin making your own movement and sound'	This provides an opportunity to be a part of the group
'Try to keep in mind that we are making a large piece of machinery'	Continuous re-focusing of the purpose of the exercise helps those who have a short attention span

Discussion topics
— Did the machine have a purpose, beginning or end?
— Did it produce anything and, if so, what?
— Is it important that we associate with other people and work together?
— Do we need to link up with people in our lives and, if so, in what situations is it appropriate?
— How does it feel to be physically close to other people?
— Is it easy or difficult to be close to others?

Variations

Allow 1 hour Personal symbols

This exercise is a projective technique through which a person is able to see more clearly some of the basic beliefs that he holds about himself.[1]

Recommended for these problems

Model of human occupation	Life-style performance model

Vol. – limited self-concept
     – decreased belief in personal effectiveness
Perf. – difficulty initiating social interaction
	Psyc. – loss of self-esteem
	     – lowered ability to assess personal skills
	Intp. – limited interpersonal skills

Stage of group development Because some self-disclosure is needed, this exercise is best done with individuals who have formed some degree of trust.

Synopsis In this exercise, each person discovers, in a random pattern they create, personal symbols whose qualities they compare to their own personalities.[2]

Materials and equipment Chairs around a table
White paper
Coloured felt pens.

Procedure

Invite the group members to help themselves to paper and felt pens. Suggest they choose a colour most relevant to their present mood	To help alleviate anxiety by taking an active role in choosing to participate

1. This exercise created by Lily Jaffe, OTR was experienced by E. Storch in one of her workshops in Vancouver, Canada, 1983.
2. A variation of this exercise is to use objects, e.g. stones, shells, flowers, etc., found either by the group at the start of the session or by the leader prior to the session. Individuals are asked to choose an object that they are attracted to, to handle that object, noticing colour, shape, texture, function, etc. and to list those qualities. The remainder of the exercise is the same as the above.

Give the following instructions:
'Imagine an ant wandering all over your sheet of paper; make a line that shows what sort of track he would make. Let him go aimlessly, doubling back on his path when you want him to, and fill the entire sheet of paper'

When all the members have completed this part, ask them to survey this pattern by half closing their eyes, thus allowing familiar or unfamiliar shapes to evolve, e.g. faces, people, animals, things, etc.	To help them shift into a different state of awareness
Encourage them not to worry if the object only slightly resembles something or is a part of something	To help those who may have difficulty with such a loose association of their vague shapes with precise images
Ask them now to: 'Use a colour to trace the outlines of these objects; to put eyes, a nose, a mouth, ears, hair, or a tail for easier identification as well as permit yourself to modify the outlines to make them more relevant to your image'	To help them make a physical decision and commitment when identifying various shapes. To make identification of the shapes quicker when discussing them later with the group
Then say: 'Now look at each shape that you have outlined and ask yourself — what qualities or characteristics does it have. List these on the back of the paper'	
Invite a volunteer to identify his images.[3] When he talks about the qualities expressed in the drawing, suggest that he consider the possibility that some of these might apply to him	To make it possible for the individual to choose whether or not he wants to identify with some of any of the qualities attributed to the image. He may in fact identify with more than he wished to reveal to the group
Ask questions when the personal beliefs are unclear. Do not assume or interpret for them connections between the object and themselves[4]	

Discussion topics   — Are we more attracted to things or people who have similar qualities to ourselves?
— People are often more intolerant of faults in others than they are of their own.
— Note the adjectives you frequently use to describe things and see if they reflect your current mood.

---

3. In reviewing the group, it will become evident that each person expressed one or two basic beliefs about himself that will be keys to his relationship with others.
4. For example, if a depressed person outlines a shoe, he may say he always tried to fit into his father's shoes, i.e. take the same career as his father, rather than your interpretation that he felt downtrodden.

Playing a sport together

Allow 10 minutes

This is an exercise to help a person develop his ability to communicate an idea nonverbally.[1, 2]

Recommended for these problems

Model of human occupation	Life-style performance model	

Vol. – inhibited self-expression due to decreased expectations of success
  – diminished sense of personal effectiveness
Perf. – deficiency in neurological skills as indicated by poverty of ideas
  – impairment of interpersonal communication skills
	Sens/mo. – limited visual-motor integration
	Cog. – poverty of ideas
	Psyc. – loss of self-reliance
	  – inhibited self-expression
	Intp. – limited interpersonal skills	

Stage of group development The exercise is appropriate to use with a group whose members can benefit from mutual support.

Synopsis This is a *theatre game* in which one team pretends to be playing a particular sport. The other team tries to identify the sport.

Materials and equipment None
Use a spacious, carpeted room.

---

1. A variation of this exercise is 'Eating a food together'. The team decides what type of food they are going to eat and then mimes the act of preparing and eating it. Again this is done with each person working independently, but at the same time. Side-coaching includes such instructions as:
   smell the food
   put it in your mouth
   chew it
   feel its texture
   taste it
   swallow it, and then react with a sound to what you have just swallowed.
2. The exercise is suitable for *videotaping*. The replay can be watched just for the fun of it or it can be used to see what players were able to mime really effectively and why. What was it about their nonverbal communication that was innovative? Sometimes after watching a tape players may wish to do the exercise again to try out and practise new ideas. This can also be taped so that participants can then see whether they were able to effect any changes.

Procedure

Invite the players to divide into two equal teams.[3]
(Call the teams *A* and *B*)

Explain the exercise as follows:
'One team (e.g. *A*) takes the *stage* while the other
team (in this case *B*) forms the audience and
sits down'

'Participants in Team *A* decide amongst themselves on a particular sport[4] they are going to play'	This gives each team member an opportunity to give ideas and cooperate with the others in coming to an agreement

---

'Then, with each person working independently
but simultaneously, the team members imagine
they are participating in the sport and show their
actions in mime'

'Team *B* watches the action of team *A* and tries
to guess the sport they chose'

Side-coaching can be given by the therapist or
a group member to assist the performers

'The teams then change places and Team *B*
takes the *stage*'

Variations

---

3. See reference to teams in the chapter entitled *Some basic concepts*, p. 21.
4. The therapist should have a few ideas prepared in case the teams need suggestions.

Rhythm circle (warm-up)

Allow 5–10 minutes

This is a *warm-up* technique designed to assist group members to learn each other's names. The exercise will also help improve concentration, psychomotor coordination and sense of rhythm.

Recommended for these problems

Model of human occupation		Life-style performance model	
Vol.	– loss of internal locus of control as indicated by lack of interaction with the environment	Sens/mo.	– slowed sensory-motor output
			– aphasia
Perf.	– impairment of interpersonal/communication as indicated by social isolation	Cog.	– short attention span
	– decreased concentration (5 minutes or less)	Psyc.	– difficulty sustaining contact with external stimuli
	– loss of vocabulary, e.g. aphasia	Intp.	– limited social interaction
	– slowing of perceptual-motor skills		

Stage of group development This exercise is good for an incohesive group in which the participants do not know each other's names and are mutually disinterested.[1]

Synopsis This is a *theatre game* consisting of a rhythmic sequential action co-ordinated with the calling of a person's name.

Materials and equipment None.

Procedure

Ask the group members to kneel on the floor in a circle and then in turn to introduce themselves by name	The circle formation means that each person is within the vision of every other person
Demonstrate the rhythm as you give the instructions	To make the exercise easier to learn

---

1. This is a good introductory exercise to use when new members join a group.

Start by giving the following instructions:
'We will learn the rhythm first. To the count of six and using both hands ...
Slap your knees, twice (*one, two*)
Clap your hands together, twice (*three, four*)
Snap your fingers, once with the right hand and once with the left hand (*five, six*)'

This requires concentration, coordination and a sense of rhythm

---

'We shall repeat the sequence from the beginning many times, trying to maintain an even pace'

This will help those whose concentration and immediate recall is rather poor

---

Continue practising until everyone can remember the actions and do them in time with one another. (The speed must be relative to that of the slowest person)

To reinforce the learning and promote a sense of individual and group achievement

---

'Now we have learned the actions, at the same time as everyone snaps their fingers, one player will call out his own name twice'

This part of the exercise can be used to encourage each person to speak up loudly and distinctly

---

'We must all help to keep the rhythm going and ...

Encourage the group members to be supportive of the caller, so that if he becomes muddled he can join in with the rhythm again

---

'while everyone snaps their fingers again, the same player will call out the name of another person twice'

Using a person's name necessitates recognising that person and making eye-contact with him

---

'The named person than takes over, firstly calling his own name twice and then that of yet another person (always in time to the finger snapping part of the rhythm) and so on'[2, 3]

The repetitive nature of the game should assist the people to learn and remember each other's names

---

Variations

---

2. As practice tends to make the participants more proficient, this exercise can be successfully used on a regular basis.
3. This exercise is contraindicated for overactive patients as it is too stimulating.

Salad
(warm-up)

Allow 10 minutes

This is a *warm-up* technique which encourages body contact and concentration.

Recommended for these problems

Model of human occupation	Life-style performance model

Vol. – feelings of powerlessness over personal actions resulting in apathy
    – decreased belief in self as indicated by difficulty in social interactions
Perf. – decreased concentration (5 minutes or less)
    – slowing of perceptual-motor skills
	Sens/mo. – slowed sensory motor output
	Cog. – short attention span
	Psyc. – apathy
	Intp. – limited interpersonal skills

Stage of group development   Use this exercise at the beginning of any group in which the members have great difficulty communicating with one another and in which the general mood is one of lethargy.

Synopsis   Two players exchange seats when their *names* are called, while the caller attempts to sit in one of their vacated chairs.

Materials and equipment   Chairs in a circle
Have one less chair than the number of people in the group.

Procedure

Have each person choose a vegetable[1, 2, 3]

---

1. For people whose concentration is very poor allow each person to write the vegetable he has chosen on a piece of paper and then pin it to his chest. An alternative to this would be to list the vegetables chosen on a blackboard, as a reference list for the centre person.
2. Vegetables, fruits, flowers, numbers or letters of the alphabet.
3. Every person should choose to be a different vegetable, i.e. no duplication.

Explain that the game will begin with one person standing in the centre of the group. He will call out two vegetables and those two people must exchange places. He will try to sit in a seat vacated by one or other of them. If he succeeds, the person left standing is the next person to call out two vegetables. The caller also has the choice of calling out 'Salad', in which case everyone must change places

Success at this game requires a fair amount of concentration and quick movements

Discussion topics — While the players are catching their breath, and before the next exercise a light-hearted discussion could be started about why individuals chose to be represented by their particular vegetable.

Variations

Allow 1 hour # Security

This is an exercise to help an individual to identify factors that promote and factors that inhibit a feeling of security.[1]

Recommended for these problems

Model of human occupation	Life-style performance model
Vol. – diminished sense of personal effectiveness	Cog. – difficulty problem-solving
Hab. – loss of identity as indicated by role imbalance	Psyc. – loss of self-reliance
Perf. – inability to problem-solve	Intp. – limited social interaction
– impairment of interpersonal communication skills	

Stage of group development This exercise is most effective and successful with a group in which the members show some degree of interest in each other.

Synopsis Each person depicts diagrammatically factors that bring security and insecurity, using a circle format; then attitudinal changes are discussed.

Materials and equipment White paper
Pencils
Chairs around a table.

Procedure

Discuss briefly the role security plays in both physical and mental well being; its connection with stress, decision-making, and relationships	To help individuals begin to look at the importance security plays in their lives
Beforehand draw a heavy black circle approximately 12 cm in diameter in the centre of a 21 × 27 cm page. Make enough copies for the group	The circle is an unconscious symbol of security or wholeness.[2] Working inside it visually elicits the feelings that are the subject of this exercise

1. Created by E. Storch, 1985.
2. Jung, Carl G. (1968) *Man and his symbols*, p. 240. New York: Doubleday and Co.

Distribute the paper and pencils then describe the exercise as follows:
'Think about those things in your life that make you feel secure and that bring you a sense of stability. Write or draw these things, whether they are people, objects or ideas, inside the circle ...
Now recall those things that bring a feeling of uneasiness and insecurity and add those outside the circle'

When everyone has completed his diagram, ask for a volunteer to share his with the group. As he describes both sets of factors suggest that he consider any relationship between the two, for example, parenting can bring both security and insecurity

Discuss amongst the group any changes that can be suggested to move items to inside the circle

To help some group members discover that factors causing insecurity can also bring security, depending on their attitude

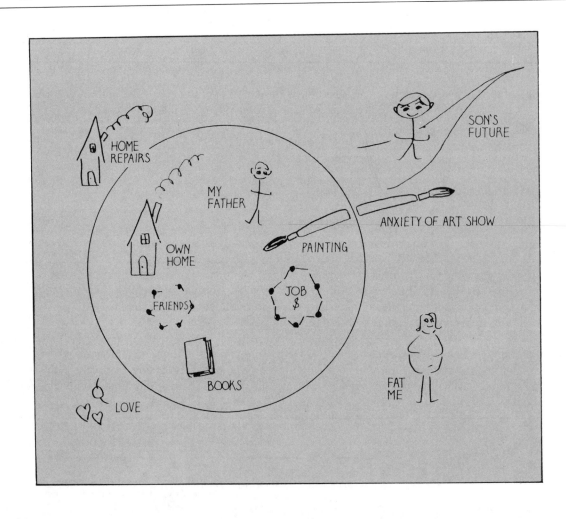

Self-portrait

Allow 1½ hours

This is an exercise in self-awareness and expression of feelings.

Recommended for these problems

Model of human occupation	Life-style performance model

Vol. – limited self-concept
   – distorted body image
   – loss of internal locus of control as indicated by
   difficulty differentiating feelings
	Sens/mo. – distorted body image
	Psyc. – lowered ability to assess personal skills
	   – difficulty understanding and expressing feelings

Stage of group development   The exercise is only appropriate when the group members have developed some degree of trust for one another.

Synopsis   *Self-portrait* is a technique during which each person in the group has his body outlined on a large sheet of paper. He is asked to paint within the outline to show how he feels today and is then invited to discuss the painting that results.

Materials and equipment[1]   Roll of 1 m wide paper
Water colour paints
Large paint brushes (e.g. 2.5 cm decorator brushes)[2]
Water containers
Water
Overalls
Felt pens
Newspapers
Masking tape
Use a large room with a sink unit in it and preferably no other furniture.

---

1. To promote a sense of responsibility, ask some or all of the group members to collect and return the materials needed, to prepare the room and to assist the less able participants.
2. To promote more spontaneity, provide larger paint brushes and reduce the time allotted for the portrait painting. This will also give additional time for discussion.

Procedure

Instruct each person as follows: 'Tear off a sheet of paper which is taller than yourself'	The gross movement occurring tends to be tension reducing, which helps to prepare the person for freer movements when he is painting. An estimation of his own height is required
'Place this sheet of paper on the floor and lie on it, finding the position in which you are most comfortable and entirely relaxed'	This encourages each person to relax and be calm. The therapist can assess each person's ability to follow the instructions
'Let me know when you are comfortable' Using a felt pen, draw around the first person who says he is comfortable, making an outline of his body	To encourage self-awareness and decision-making
Invite this person to take the marker and draw around another person who says he is ready, and so on until each person has been outlined[3]	This task requires coordination and physical contact with another person. It may also increase awareness of body image through the sense of touch
Continue with the following instructions: 'Show how you feel, right now, by painting inside your own outline'	This allows each person to express how he is feeling, graphically, and encourages him to search and identify the emotions inside him
'Use different colours for the different feelings you are experiencing'	More than one feeling may be expressed by saying this
'Do *not* depict the clothes you are wearing'	To discourage a concrete response
'Try to be finished in 15 minutes'	This is to encourage uninhibited expression by each person and aid in the therapist's assessment of the ability to complete a task within a given time. The therapist should also observe such aspects as colour choice, manner of application and interaction
When the time allowance is up invite each person to explain the feelings he has portrayed in his painting (see Self-portrait, p. 121)	To assist the person to communicate his feelings verbally using the nonverbal material as a reference
Encourage discussion about the portraits by the group	This is to develop awareness of other people and their feelings, and encourage the participants to check the accuracy of their perceptions

3. If the group is large or the attention span of the members short, ask them to choose a partner and outline each other. This will ensure that the outlining part of the activity takes a shorter period of time.

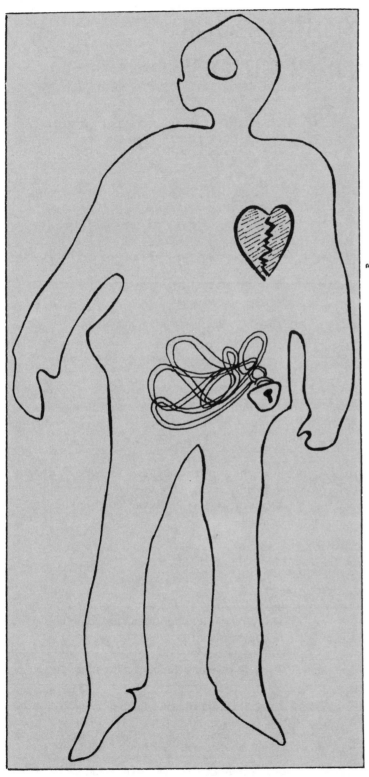

"THIS SHOWS A LARGE EMPTY AREA
IN MY HEAD, AND MY STOMACH
IS TIED UP IN KNOTS, PADLOCKED
BUT I CAN'T FIND THE KEY...
I FEEL DETACHED FROM MY
FAMILY... I FEEL I DO
EVERYTHING IN A MECHANICAL
WAY"

SELF-PORTRAIT

Simultaneous conversations

Allow 5–10 minutes

This is an exercise in self-assertion. It takes the form of a *theatre game*.[1]

Recommended for these problems

Model of human occupation	Life-style performance model
Vol. – impairment of interpersonal communication as indicated by decreased eye contact Perf. – difficulty speaking voluntarily due to decrease in spontaneous psychomotor behaviour – unassertive in social interaction – decreased concentration (5–15 minutes)	Sens/mo. – limited spontaneous conversation Cog. – short attention span Intp. – fear of eye contact – decreased assertiveness in social situations

Stage of group development The group members should be familiar enough with each other that they can all risk being assertive in a supportive environment.

Synopsis Two players sit opposite one another and are assigned to be either *for* or *against* a designated topic. Then, at the same time and maintaining eye-contact, they talk at one another, *without* responding to any part of their opponent's monologue.

Materials and equipment None

Procedure

Invite two players to sit facing one another ...	This provides an opportunity for volunteers to come forward
and to make eye-contact	To assist concentration upon the other person

---

1. The exercise is suitable for *videotaping*. The replay can be watched just for fun or to look at the specifics of being assertive. These would be such things as being able to maintain eye-contact, talk at a reasonably even pace, talk quite loudly, think quickly and creatively and not opt-out of the game in any way. The nonverbal behaviour of participants can also be observed. The therapist can help the players become aware of how to reinforce what they have to say by using appropriate body positions, gestures and facial expression.

The remainder of the group forms the audience	To provide a sense of 'theatre'
Ask the audience to name a topic[2] (the more ridiculous it is the more amusing the exercise) . . .	To encourage a sense of involvement on everyone's part and promote enjoyment
and assign[3] one of the players to be *for* it and the other to be *against*	
Explain the exercise to the players as follows: 'The object of this game is to defend your assigned stand, using all the arguments you can possibly think of and to *avoid* responding to *any* of your opponent's monologue.[4] You do this by talking *at* one another simultaneously'	To provide an opportunity for self-assertion and to encourage increased concentration and extemporaneous speech
'Try to keep looking each other in the eye all the time'	To encourage the ability to follow one train of thought without being easily distracted
'The players will start speaking when I signal, and . . .	
'you, the audience are the *jury*'	
'Listen carefully to their conversations and if either of them hesitates, answers his opponent's monologue, or stops speaking altogether, call out, because he is the loser'	To encourage concentration and a sense of participation on the part of the audience
The game then continues with either the loser being replaced by the person who noticed his mistake or another pair of players with the same or a new topic	To enable all the participants to have an opportunity of experiencing the exercise
A discussion at the end may be appropriate[5]	To assist self-awareness and expression of feelings evoked by the exercise

2. In case the group is not forthcoming with any suggestions the therapist should be prepared with some alternatives (see Suggestions at the end of the exercise).
3. It may assist players who are not very self-assured if they are able to choose whether to be *for* or *against*. This is because it is often easier to defend something one believes in and has chosen to support.
4. As the players become more familiar with the exercise, encourage them to force their opponent to respond by such ruses as questions, gesticulations, laughter, etc.
5. During discussion it may be appropriate to point out that this game does not approximate to normal conversation where it is always important to listen and respond to another person. However, the exercise may highlight some of the frustration that can be felt when one's conversation is ignored. It will also reinforce the importance of maintaining eye-contact when trying to keep another person interested in what one has to say and provide a chance to practise being assertive.

Discussion topics — What did the group members think about the exercise?
— How did it make them feel?
— What does being assertive mean?
— How can a person be assertive?
— What nonverbal behaviours help a person be assertive?
— How does this exercise differ from normal interaction?

Suggestions for 'Simultaneous conversations'

Jelly beans
Bottle tops
Doughnuts
Television
Pornography
High-rise buildings
Gardening
Dates
Comedians
Rubber bands

Garbage cans
Politicians
Clouds
Cigarettes
Milk
Log cabins
Newspapers
Chewing gum
Banana skins
Secondhand shoes

Variations

Allow 1 hour or more # Soapbox debate

This is an exercise to help individuals feel more comfortable when speaking in a group. It encourages decision-making and reasoning in a clear logical manner.[1]

Recommended for these problems

Model of human occupation	Life-style performance model
Vol. – decreased belief in self as indicated by difficulty talking in a group situation – diminished sense of personal effectiveness Perf. – deficiencies in process skills as indicated by: difficulty formulating opinions difficulty planning	Cog. – difficulty making choices Psyc. – loss of self-reliance – fear of risking personal opinions Intp. – limited skills in verbal group interaction

Stage of group development   The exercise should be used at a stage in group development when the participants feel fairly comfortable with one another.[2]

Synopsis   This exercise takes the form of a modified debate. Each person, in turn, makes a decision *for* or *against* a set topic and then supports his/her decision with three reasons. No one else may voice his/her opinion until the speaker has finished and throws the topic open for debate.[3, 4]

---

1. Created by E. Storch, 1970.
2. It is contraindicated for the physically overactive patient.
3. The exercise allows each person to express opinions that he may have held when he was functioning healthily and when he relied on his own judgement. It involves short periods of concentration (while listening to the speaker) alternated with an opportunity for the expression of thoughts. It is, therefore, a useful exercise for listening, thinking and speaking.
4. The exercise can be videotaped. The replay can be used to look carefully at whether the participants were able to make decisions, formulate opinions and present their reasons clearly. Poor speaking habits, such as mumbling, talking very softly, talking very loudly, talking very fast or in a very hesitant way, will also become apparent. The observations made while watching the tape can form the basis for a discussion.

Materials and equipment   Chairs around a table
Prepared slips of paper[5] (or paper and pencils)
A container (hat, box, etc.).

Procedure

Before beginning the exercise, list a number of controversial issues on separate slips of paper.[6] Word each one so that it can be answered by 'Yes' or 'No'. For example: 'Do you believe that there should be a minimum drinking age in pubs?'	The issues can be chosen to suit the group, but should relate to current events (as found in local/ national newspapers). This will encourage contact with the world outside the hospital. Be aware that clear wording of each question will assist the speaker to think more clearly
Invite the group to sit around a table	This gives the group a comfortable 'boardroom' atmosphere
Explain the exercise as follows: 'Each person will have a chance to be on the soapbox'	To raise self-esteem, as each person will be listened to by the group
'You will take a topic out of the hat . . .	This freedom of choice may discourage the suspicious person from thinking that the topic was specifically written for him
and decide whether you are *for* or *against* it'	To give an opportunity for decision-making
'Read the topic to us, tell us whether you agree or disagree with it and then back up your decision with three reasons'[7]	This gives each person a structure around which to organise his thoughts and communicate them clearly
In this exercise, the therapist has two jobs: (1) maintaining the freedom of speech for the speakers when necessary and (2) restating clearly what the speaker has said (if he has combined his three points into one sentence or if he has rambled	To show the individual he has the right to speak no matter how difficult it is for him To give him a chance to hear his thoughts clearly stated and to give him the positive feedback that he has been understood

5. Decide whether you or the group members are to prepare the topics for discussion. This will depend on how inventive the group members can be in their choice of issues. If this task is given to the group members it may encourage them to show an active interest in community affairs (see Suggestions at the end of the exercise).
6. Issues which are non-threatening and of an impersonal nature are easiest for discussion. Select the types of issues in relation to the group's overall capability in handling them.
7. It may be appropriate to give each person a pencil and a slip of paper on which to note his points.

When the speaker has finished open the topic for debate	This will encourage an interchange of ideas between two or more individuals who may otherwise find spontaneous conversation difficult
Move on to the next person after a maximum of ten minutes[8, 9]	To allow time for each person to take his turn

Discussion topics
— Why is it important to be able to make decisions?
— What are some of the problems caused by being indecisive?
— How easy or difficult was it to formulate opinions?
— What happens in a conversation when everyone is in agreement?
— What happens in a conversation when people have differing opinions?

Suggestions for 'Soapbox debate' topics
— Will it rain tomorrow?
— Should cars be kept out of the city centre?
— Is a welfare state essential?
— Should cigarette advertising be banned?
— Man must work to enjoy his leisure.
— Is space research important?
— The monarchy is essential for a democratic state.
— Cars should be limited to one per household.
— Strikes are more effective than bargaining.

Variations

---

8. When there are verbose and/or hyperactive members, or if the group is large, it may be advisable to limit both the speaker's time and the open debate.
9. Do not distribute all the topics at the start, or you may find some people unable to listen to the speaker as they are concerned about how to defend their own topic best.

Story, story

Allow 10–30 minutes

This is an exercise to help individuals feel more confident speaking, without any preparation, to a group of people.[1]

Recommended for these problems

Model of human occupation		Life-style performance model	
Vol.	– diminished sense of personal effectiveness	Sens/mo. –	limited spontaneous conversation
Perf.	– decrease in spontaneous psychomotor behaviour as indicated by difficulty speaking spontaneously	Cog.	– short attention span
	– decreased concentration (5–15 minutes)		– poverty of ideas
	– deficiency in neurological skills as indicated by poverty of ideas	Psyc.	– loss of self-reliance

Stage of group development   This exercise is best used in a group that has developed some unity and where the members are actively participating to the best of their abilities.

Synopsis   This is a *theatre game* in which a group of players tell a story. Each player speaks in turn, trying to keep the story coherent and grammatically correct. If, however, someone makes a mistake then the story stops while this particular player mimes his own death and then joins the audience.

Materials and equipment   None
Use a familiar room.

Procedure

Invite from four to seven[2] players to form a line ...   This provides an opportunity for volunteers to come forward[3]

---

1. This exercise can be *videotaped*. The replay can be watched just for fun or to look more specifically at some of the difficulties participants encountered. These might be such things as not being able to think of anything to say, difficulty paying attention and not speaking audibly.
2. Since this exercise is dependent upon there being enough people to be both *story tellers* and *audience*, the number of *story tellers* should be no more than half the group.
3. Depending on the degree of response the therapist may need to encourage or even choose *story tellers*.

in front of the audience . . .	To promote a sense of *theatre*
and one person to be the *Director*[4]	
Explain the exercise as follows: The audience chooses a *hero* about whom the players are going to tell a story	This encourages audience participation
The *Director* then says, 'The *hero* of your story is . . .' and points to one of the players, who immediately begins to make up a story about the designated hero	This person is encouraged to speak spontaneously
The player continues with his story until the *Director* points to a different player (the game is more entertaining if the switch occurs while the person speaking is in the middle of a sentence)	
This person takes the story up where the previous speaker left off and so the game continues	
The only rules are that the story must be grammatically correct and coherent	This means that the players need to listen very carefully as well as concentrate upon the *Director*
It is the responsibility of the audience to edit the story, that is, to listen for any grammatical mistakes, repeated words, etc. and as soon as they hear one to cry, 'Die'	The continuous audience participation in this way requires concentration and active involvement in the game
At this point the story stops,[5] while the player who made the error mimes his own death[6] and then joins the audience	To encourage self-expression and provide an opportunity to be entertaining
The *Director*, repeating the last word that was spoken, points to another player and the story continues until one player is left	To refresh the players' memories

---

4. Initially it may be advisable for the therapist to take this role, thereby demonstrating how to direct the game and promote enjoyment. A withdrawn person might be encouraged to participate as the *Director's assistant* and select the speakers.
5. The *Director* must remember the last word spoken.
6. It is best if the leader mimes a few examples of entertaining deaths before the game starts, stressing that the action should be exaggerated and funny. Encourage the audience to applaud the player when he finishes his mime. We are aware that some therapists may view this part of the exercise as threatening and/or untherapeutic. Although suicidal thoughts or attempts are experienced by many patients, they are infrequently discussed in a group setting. This exercise does not presume to promote discussion about suicide: it merely attempts to encourage expression of death in a nonverbal and entertaining way. We recommend that the therapist assesses whether the group can cope with this but not to underestimate their ability or allow her own anxiety to be the deciding factor. In practice we found that the participants react to the exercise according to how it is presented.

This person concludes the story with a moral
and is either applauded or asked to 'Die',
depending on whether his moral is accepted
or rejected by the audience

The game can be continued with a new set
of players and a new *hero*

Invite discussion at the end

Discussion topics   — Discuss any feelings that were evoked by having to speak up in
front of a group.
— Discuss the effect of audience participation, laughter and
applause upon the story-tellers.
— Discuss feelings evoked by miming death.

THE PLAYER WHO
MADE THE ERROR
MIMES HIS OWN
DEATH

Variations

Story-telling

Allow 1 hour

This is an exercise to help individuals feel more comfortable speaking out in a group. It encourages creative thinking. It is a projective technique.

Recommended for these problems

Model of human occupation	Life-style performance model
Vol. – decreased belief in self as indicated by difficulty with public speaking – diminished sense of personal effectiveness as indicated by low self-confidence Perf. – difficulty initiating social interaction – depression as indicated by psychomotor retardation – deficiency in process skills as indicated by difficulty formulating ideas	Cog. – poverty of ideas Psyc. – loss of self-reliance – depression Intp. – limited skills in verbal group interaction – limited ability to initiate conversation

Stage of group development

This exercise can be used at any stage of group cohesion.

Synopsis

In this exercise the participants create and relate a simple story once they have been given a visual inspiration and structured guidelines.

Materials and equipment

Magazine pictures
Chairs around a table.

Procedure

Before beginning the exercise, collect from magazines pictures that show some action taking place, preferably where some ambiguity exists so that the situation could have more than one interpretation	
Invite the group to sit around the table and explain the purpose of the exercise	To encourage group cohesion and eliminate the anxiety of the unknown

Begin the exercise as follows:
'On the table are an assortment of pictures from magazines. Choose one that appeals to you'

The choice of picture will reflect how he is feeling at this time

'Look carefully at it and decide three things: What is happening now in the picture, what happened before the picture was taken, and what will happen afterwards'[1]

This gives each person a structure to assist him to organize his thoughts and communicate them clearly

Each person is then asked in turn to tell his story. Questions from the group are encouraged

To help those with a poverty of ideas to elaborate on their story

Repeat this procedure with a new picture and story if desired[2]

Variations

---

1. In reviewing this group it will become evident that what each person expressed in his story is a major issue that he is concerned with at the present time. The issue will become quickly apparent if two or more stories are chosen.
2. A variation can be added if time allows. The group as a whole choose one picture by voting. Then a continuous story is created by each person, in turn around the table, adding on another episode until the group decides that the story is finished. It is a useful assessment tool for memory and concentration, as names, ages, and events must be remembered.

Support systems

Allow 1 hour

This is an exercise to help an individual to identify his existing support system and then to analyse its effectiveness.[1]

Recommended for these problems

Model of human occupation	Life-style performance model
Vol. – limited self-concept Hab. – inadequate support system – lack of identity due to role loss Perf. – difficulty initiating social interaction – decreased social involvement	Psyc. – lowered ability to assess personal skills Intp. – withdrawal from reciprocal interpersonal relationships – limited interpersonal skills

Stage of group development   This exercise is most effective and successful with a group in which the members show some degree of interest in each other.

Synopsis   Each person makes a simple collage which depicts his/her support system. The individuals within the system are identified and their relationship to the key person is defined.

Materials and equipment   Magazines
Glue
Scissors
Large sheets of paper
Tables and chairs

Procedure

Before handing out any of the materials explain the exercise as follows:

To catch the attention of the easily distracted individuals before they become engrossed in their magazines
To state the therapeutic purpose clearly before any deprecatory ideas associated with kindergarten materials emerge

1. Created by E. Storch, 1981.

'Think about the people (friends and relations) who are important to you. The people to whom you turn when you are happy or sad, lonely or confused, for conversation or entertainment'

'Look fairly quickly through the magazines and cut out pictures that represent these people. Do not concern yourself with likenesses'	To allow the unconscious a chance to guide the choice and to discourage conscious reasoning
'Find a picture to represent yourself as well'	This choice may prove to be quite revealing to both the participant and the therapist
'Glue this picture on to the centre of your paper'	
'Then place your friends and relatives around you. Put those to whom you feel closest near or touching you on the paper and represent the distance you feel from the others by the distance they are placed from your picture in the centre'	The spatial relationship used symbolically to represent an emotional relationship is a simple nonverbal tool that bypasses cognition

Hand out the supplies and restate the instructions
for anyone who had difficulty following them
When most people have finished ask:
'Does anyone need more time?'

Allow time for the members and yourself to
explain their collages
Encourage the group members to ask questions
of one another

Discussion topics   — The different roles family members play in our lives.
— The tendency to rely on one person rather than a number of
people.
— The use of professionals and community facilities and services in
a support system.

Variations

The chair

Allow 10–30 minutes

This is an exercise in spontaneous self-expression and social inter-action. It takes the form of a *theatre game.*[1]

Recommended for these problems

Model of human occupation	Life-style performance model
Vol. – diminished sense of personal effectiveness as indicated by low self-confidence Perf. – impairment of interpersonal communication as indicated by social anxiety – unassertive in social interaction – decrease in psychomotor behaviour as indicated by difficulty speaking voluntarily	Psyc. – loss of self reliance – feelings of anxiety Intp. – decreased assertiveness in social situations – limited spontaneous conversation

Stage of group development It is recommended that this exercise be done with a group whose members are well enough acquainted that they feel safe to improvise.

Synopsis A player from the group initiates and develops a skit with an opponent who is seated in a chair. The purpose of the skit is to persuade the opponent to get up from his seat.

Materials and equipment Chair
Use a familiar room that is quiet.

Procedure

Invite the players to sit in a large circle on the floor and to find comfortable positions	To encourage everyone to be relaxed and, thereby, make participation in the exercise easier
Create a *centre stage* by placing a chair in the middle of the circle and ...	

1. The exercise is suitable for *videotaping.* The replay will be fun to watch for all members. The participants will be able to view their abilities to speak spontaneously, to be assertive, or to be persuasive.

ask if there is a volunteer who would like to sit in the chair	To provide an opportunity for a member to choose to be the centre of attention
Explain the exercise as follows: 'The object of this game is to persuade the person in the chair to get up from it. You may use any means to achieve this, apart from moving the chair or physical force'	
'Any player may approach[2] the person in the chair and . . .	To encourage spontaneous participation
'through his actions and/or conversation set the scene'[3]	To provide an opportunity for self-expression
'The two of them converse until the seated player is finally persuaded to stand up'	To assist the formation of a brief relationship with another person and to practise communication with him
'Other players may join in the conversation at any point if they wish to'	This freedom allows individuals from the audience to support and encourage the players by spontaneously participating with them
'Once the seated player does stand up he re-joins the circle. His opponent, taking the seat, waits to be approached by another player who starts a new skit'[4]	To allow as many players as possible the chance to participate, especially those who are shy or self-conscious and require some encouragement
Audience participation should be encouraged at all times (i.e. laughter, applause, verbal encouragement, etc.)	To involve the maximum number of people

2. Unless the players are very self-confident, it is likely they will hesitate in coming forward initially. Since this is an exercise in spontaneity, we do not suggest that specific people are asked to participate, rather that the leader demonstrates the game using very ordinary familiar scenes (see Suggestions at the end of the exercise). In this way the group members can be encouraged to feel safe enough to act out their own ideas.
3. For example: a player may approach the person in the chair walking like an old man and make a comment that sets the scene of a bus; or he may walk briskly and say, 'Good morning, madam. Is there a particular shoe that interests you?', thereby setting the scene in a shoe shop.
4. As the game continues, encourage the person in the chair to be more reluctant to give up his position. This will allow the players to be more subtle and skilful in their handling of the situation.

Suggestions for 'The chair'   Choose situations which are familiar, easy to enact and naturally require that one of the participants is seated. They should also lend themselves to comedy and improvisation.

— Buying a pair of shoes in a shoe store
— Two people sitting in a doctor or dentist's waiting room
— Finding yourself in someone else's seat at the theatre
— Travelling on the bus when a pregnant or heavily laden lady gets on
— Eating dinner at a restaurant and the waiter spills the soup
— Sitting in the cockpit of an aircraft that is about to crash
— Sitting on a park bench enjoying the sunshine

Variations

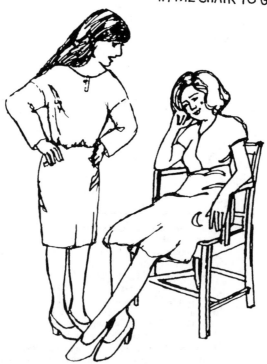

PERSUADE THE PERSON IN THE CHAIR TO GET UP

The matchbox is ...? (warm-up)

Allow 10–30 minutes

This is an exercise to develop the capacity to be observant and use words that are descriptive. It can be used as a *warm-up* technique or as a longer exercise if required.

Recommended for these problems

Model of human occupation	Life-style performance model
Vol. – decreased belief in self as indicated by difficulty talking in a group situation – loss of internal locus of control as indicated by lack of interaction with the environment Perf. – neurological deficiencies as indicated by visual-motor deficits	Sens/mo. – decreased visual/tactile discrimination Psyc. – difficulty sustaining contact with external stimuli Intp. – limited skills in verbal group interaction

Stage of group development

This exercise could be used with a group of very withdrawn patients to help them to stay in touch with their immediate situation and begin to communicate. If the exercise is used in this way the time allowance should be extended until the level of participation indicates that progression to another exercise is appropriate.

Synopsis

An article is passed around and as each person receives it he is invited to contribute one thing towards its description.

Materials and equipment

Small objects, such as pencil, ashtray, key, vase, jar, etc. Use a small familiar room.

Procedure

Invite the group members to sit in a circle

Explain the exercise as follows:
'I am going to pass a small *article*, (e.g. a matchbox)
around the group'[1]

---

1. These articles can be collected beforehand or each person can be asked to produce something he has on him at the time.

'When each person receives it, he is invited to describe something about the *article*[2] before passing it on to the next person'	To improve observation skills and to encourage the individual to say what he sees, or feels This not only enables everyone to participate but the process of handing the object on encourages each person to relate to his neighbour
'The object of the game is to describe as many aspects of the *article* as we can without repetition'	To encourage greater concentration and originality
Continue passing the same *article* around until all possibilities have been exhausted and then invite a group member to introduce a new *article*	This stimulates the generation of a wide variety of observations, necessitating some creative thinking. Inviting the group members to make personal contributions may encourage a greater degree of interest and participation

Variations

---

2. With patients whose thought processes are very slow it is sometimes advisable to stimulate ideas by suggestion (e.g. as to shape, size, smell, texture, weight and use). This may be done as you give the instructions or may need to be given as coaching to each person in turn.

Allow 1 hour # Theme collage

This is an exercise to promote group cohesion through the nonverbal and verbal interaction which occurs when a group of people work together.

Recommended for these problems

Model of human occupation	Life-style performance model
Vol. – impairment of interpersonal communication skills as indicated by social anxiety Hab. – feelings of incompetence Perf. – decreased social involvement – deficiency in process skills as indicated by poverty of ideas – limited task-oriented skills – difficulty planning	Cog. – poverty of ideas Psyc. – feelings of anxiety Intp. – limited interpersonal skills – withdrawal from reciprocal interpersonal relationships

Stage of group development This is a valuable exercise to use with a group that lacks cohesion and contains a number of very isolated members.

Synopsis The group choose a theme together and then compose a collage which represents each person's perception of that theme. The collage is then displayed.

Materials and equipment Magazines
Scissors
Glue and glue pots
Felt pens
Large sheet of paper
Newspaper
Use a large working table and chairs around it.

Procedure

Explain the exercise as follows:
'We are going to make a collage using magazine pictures'

'First, however, we have to choose a theme.[1] Does anyone have any suggestions?'	This part of the exercise requires a group decision which is the first step toward cohesion
'Then I would like you to go through the magazines and find pictures or examples of that theme. Cut the pictures out'	This gives each person an opportunity for self-expression and personal interpretation of the theme
Ask the first group member who appears restless to arrange the contributions for the collage on a sheet of background paper. Engage the next restless person to assist him in sticking them on[2]	Giving this job to the person who finds the first part of the exercise difficult, perhaps due to anxiety or poor concentration, will provide him with a constructive outlet for his restlessness
Make sure each group member is represented by at least one contribution	This ensures that the collage is a group product and represents each person's involvement in the task (e.g. his feelings, his past experiences, his ideas as they relate to the theme, etc.)
'When the collage is complete we will discuss the theme and the pictures that each of us chose'	To promote discussion amongst the participants
Suggest that the group hang the collage up	Once hung the collage is a visual display of the group's ability to work together

Discussion topics — How easy or difficult was it to find pictures that related to the theme?
— Why did each person choose his particular pictures?
— What were your feelings about the theme?
— How did the group work together and what part did each person play in the task?

Variations

---

1. Give a few examples for possible themes, e.g. Leisure-time, Anger, Family life, Things I have enjoyed.
2. Arranging and pasting the pictures could also be a group task requiring cooperation, compromise, decision-making and imagination on everyone's part.

Time management

Allow 1 hour

This exercise assesses use of time and encourages analysing options, for stress management.

Recommended for these problems

Model of human occupation	Life-style performance model

Vol. – loss of interest in activities
Hab. – role imbalance
     – loss of organizational skills
Perf. – depression as indicated by social isolation
     – inability to problem-solve
	Cog. – difficulty problem solving
	Psyc.– inability to manage time
	Intp. – limited interpersonal skills

Stage of group development   This exercise can be done with a group who do not know each other.

Synopsis   Each person calculates the various ways he spends his time in a 24-hour period then displays it on a pie graph.

Materials and equipment   Chairs around a table
Paper
Pencils and erasers
Coloured felt pens.

Procedure

Beforehand draw a circle, 16 cm in diameter in the bottom half of a 21 × 27 cm page. List above the circle on the lefthand side: Sleep, eating and meal preparation, etc. Divide the circle into equal sections (See diagram, page 144.) Make enough copies of this for the group

Introduce the topic of time management by talking about the importance of time planning, so as to achieve a balance of both duties and pleasures

Distribute the prepared sheets and pencils. Invite the participants to look at an average 24-hour day[1] and to calculate the time spent in the various activities listed at the top of the paper

To help each person think in terms of total time spent (e.g. with hygiene) so that he will perceive the circle as a graph and not as a 24-hour clock where activities appear periodically throughout the day

Then ask them to transfer this information onto the circle, (divided into 24 equal wedges) blocking out time in sections, e.g. 8 hours of sleep would be blocked out using 8 wedges of the circle. Suggest using a different colour for each activity as this makes it easier to see later. Move about the group assisting those who need more clarification

To help those people who have difficulty seeing things graphically

When everyone has finished suggest that they share their information, beginning with a volunteer

As each person describes his day, ask: 'What are the things you would like to include but don't have time to do?' 'Do you feel dissatisfied with the amount of time you spend in any category whether it is too much or too little?' 'Can you suggest any alternatives so that you can change what you don't like?' 'Has anyone in the group some suggestions?'

To help, for example, the workaholic make time for relaxation or the depressed mother build in time for herself amid the endless household chores

After each person has had a turn, move into a period of open discussion

Sleep
Hygiene and grooming
Eating and meal preparation
Household management
Job
Leisure time
Family life
Miscellaneous
Daydreaming

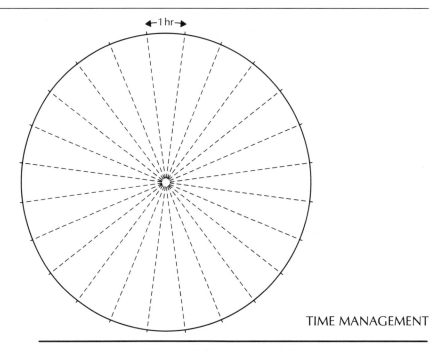

←1hr→

TIME MANAGEMENT

1. An average day outside hospital if they are currently inpatients.

Where am I?

Allow 30 minutes

This is an exercise to develop (1) awareness of oneself and others in terms of the introversion-extraversion continuum and (2) the ability to express feelings directly.

Recommended for these problems

Model of human occupation	Life-style performance model

Vol. – limited self-concept
 – loss of internal locus of control as indicated by:
  lack of insight
  difficulty differentiating feelings
Hab. – role imbalance
Perf. – unassertive in social interaction
  deficiency in processing skills affecting planning
	Cog. – difficulty making choices
	Psyc. – lowered ability to assess personal skills
	  – difficulty understanding and expressing feelings
	Intp. – decreased assertiveness in social situations

Stage of group development   This exercise may be used to stimulate a discussion[1] and is appropriate for a group that has achieved some sense of group identity. It is a valuable exercise to introduce when group energy is low.

Synopsis   Everyone is invited to stand on an imaginary line to show firstly, how he sees himself participating in the group and, secondly, how he would like to participate. Discussion is then encouraged by giving each person an opportunity to explain the positions that he took.

Materials and equipment   2 pieces of chalk, e.g. one white and one coloured
Clear enough floor space to allow everyone to stand in a line.

---

1. This exercise may be appropriate to use when participation by the majority of group members is generally passive, perhaps with the exception of one or two members who take very active roles.
   Through this technique, the quieter members are presented with an opportunity to say how they would like to participate and what is hindering them. The active ones are given a chance to explain why they are more involved.

Procedure

Invite everyone in the group to stand up	The physical movement encourages an attitude of readiness for the exercise
Explain the exercise as follows: 'I am going to call this corner of the room *outgoing, leader* and the opposite corner *withdrawn, follower*, so that these represent the extremes of possible participation in the group'	
Enquire if everyone understands	This allows anyone who was not listening to ask for the instructions to be repeated or re-phrased
'Imagine that there is a line drawn between these two corners'	
'Think about how you, personally, participate in the group and then . . .	To encourage self-awareness and . . .
'place yourself somewhere on the imaginary line to show this'	provide a chance for each person to express his conclusion nonverbally
'You will find that the position you choose is relative to those that the other people in the group choose'	To develop an increased awareness of others
'Mark your position by writing your name, using the white chalk'[2]	This will act as a visual aid in the discussion part of the exercise
'Now ask yourself if this is where you would most like to be and . . .	To encourage the individual to consider his ideal behaviour in contrast to his actual behaviour and express the former in a nonverbal way
'if it is not, then take a second position on the imaginary line, to show how you would prefer to participate'	
'If you are content with your present participation in the group then stay where you are'	This is to encourage each person to be honest
'Mark your position even if you have not moved using the coloured chalk'	

---

2. Wait until everyone has chosen and marked his/her position before proceeding with the next part of the exercise.

When everyone has done this, invite the group members to sit in a circle around the marked positions

To bring the group members into a position that is not only more conducive to discussion but also enables them to observe the positions that everyone else took

Invite each person to talk about the reasons he had for taking his particular position, or positions, along the imaginary line . . .

To encourage each person to express his ideas and feelings in a direct way

and encourage the group to discuss these

By understanding each other's behaviour the group members are likely to become more supportive of one another

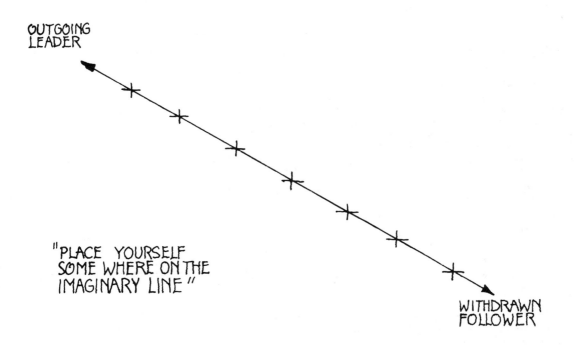

Discussion topics — How does the position each person chose relate to his/her participation in the group?
— Does each person's participation in the group have any relationship to his/her lifestyle, work, friendships, and methods of coping with problems?

Variations

Allow 1 hour or more   # Who am I?

This is an exercise in self-awareness and self-expression.

Recommended for these problems

Model of human occupation	Life-style performance model
Vol. – loss of internal locus of control as indicated by difficulty differentiating feelings – limited self-concept Hab. – role imbalance Perf. – impairment of interpersonal communication skills as indicated by social isolation – limited task orientated skills	Psyc. – difficulty understanding and expressing feelings – lowered ability to assess personal skills and limitations Intp. – limited social interaction

Stage of group development   This exercise is very appropriate to use with a group containing many new members.[1]

Synopsis   The technique takes the form of a self-portrait collage which each person makes to illustrate his personality and *life space*.[2] It is followed by an opportunity for him to explain and discuss his portrayed identity with the other group members.

Materials and equipment   Sheets of paper approximately 60 cm × 90 cm, one for each person[3]
Wide selection of magazines
Scissors
Glue
Overalls (Optional)
Use a room which has sufficient working space or tables for the number of participants.[4]

---

1. This is an excellent technique to use with patients who have recently arrived in hospital or any other treatment setting. During the course of the exercise the therapist can make a general assessment of each patient, while the patient uses the exercise to *settle in*. By recalling the familiar life away from hospital and sharing this with unfamiliar people the patient achieves some degree of comfort and personal identity.
2. Sandra Watanabe, O.T.R., *Four Concepts Basic to the Occupational Therapy Process*, American Journal of Occupational Therapy (1968) XXII, 5, p. 439.
3. Half a sheet of construction paper makes a sturdy backing and allows each person to choose a colour that reflects his personality.
4. Work on the floor to encourage a free and relaxed atmosphere.

Procedure

Explain the exercise as follows:
'We are going to make individual collages. Imagine that a friend wishes to know all about you, but you are unable to speak'

A clear explanation is needed to allay fears of having to perform and perhaps be judged

'Make a poster that illustrates your personality and life style, by selecting appropriate pictures from these magazines'

'Try to include pictures that show some of the following things about you (e.g. your attitudes and interests, likes and dislikes, characteristics, family, friends, jobs, ambitions, feelings, problems, reasons for being in hospital and so on).
Be selective because it is impossible to illustrate every aspect of yourself'[5]

To increase self-awareness and encourage appropriate selection, discrimination and coordination of pictures from a wide range of possibilities

5. Analysis of the picture selected will aid in the assessment of each person's perceptual and motor ability, mental state and life space.

'Here are the magazines and scissors.[6] Let me know when you need the background paper'[7]	To promote active participation and stimulate interest at the beginning of the exercise
'Let's complete the collage in 20 minutes'	Providing a set time in which to complete the task encourages organization in working. It also helps the overactive person control his need to be all inclusive
Besides making her own poster, the role of the therapist is to clarify the task for those who don't understand and to encourage discussion while everyone is working	
When the time is up ask, 'Does anyone need more time?'	To encourage each person to decide whether his collage is completed or not and to take responsibility for requesting more time
When all are finished, invite each person to tell the group about his collage. It is important that the therapist also talks about her own collage	To provide an opportunity to share personal information with other people and aid in the establishment and recognition of a personal identity. To provide a basis for conversation between individuals

Variations

---

6. To encourage communication and sharing, provide fewer scissors and glue pots than there are group members.
7. When working with patients with low self-esteem, who often reject activities for fear of looking foolish, present them with the scissors and magazines first of all and give them the paper and glue when it is needed. This eliminates the feelings and response of 'We're back at kindergarten,' that occurs when they are confronted with all these materials at once.

Who stole the cookie from the cookie jar? (warm-up)

Allow 5–10 minutes

This exercise is a rhythmic *warm-up* technique.

Recommended for these problems

Model of human occupation	Life-style performance model
Perf. – decreased concentration (5–15 minutes) – slowing of perceptual-motor skills – impairment of interpersonal/communication skills as indicated by social isolation	Sens/mo. – slowed sensory-motor output Cog. – short attention span Intp. – limited social interaction

Stage of group development   The exercise can be used successfully with most groups.

Synopsis   It is a *theatre game* in which words are said in time to a clapped rhythm.

Materials and equipment   Blackboard and chalk
Use a room that is spacious.

Procedure

Before the session starts, write the words to be spoken on the blackboard[1]	This is to assist anyone who has difficulty remembering them
Invite the players to kneel on the floor in a circle ...	A circle enables everyone to see everyone else and promotes a sense of wholeness

---

1. Words to be written up:
   'Who stole the cookie from the cookie jar?'
   'Was it you number ...?'
   'Who me?'
   'Yes, you.'
   'Couldn't be.'
   'Then who?'
   'Number ...'

and to number off to the right. The leader is usually Number One[2]	Encourage the players to speak up clearly, so that everyone can hear
Explain the game as follows: 'The leader claps his hands in a simple rhythm[3] which the rest of us imitate'	To do this requires concentration, motor coordination and a sense of rhythm
'Then when everyone is familiar with the rhythm the leader begins speaking in time to it, saying . . .	
'Leader: "Who stole the cookie from the cookie jar? Was it you number four?"'[4]	The exercise becomes more difficult at this point, demanding greater concentration and psychomotor coordination
'Number Four: "Who me?" Leader: "Yes, you" Number Four: "Couldn't be" Leader: "Then who?" Number Four: "Number Ten"'[5]	This provides an opportunity to practise quick verbal interaction Since the players do not know which one of them will be called next they need to remain alert
'Number Ten: "Who me?" Number Four: "Yes, you" Number Ten: "Couldn't be" and so on'	
If at any point one of the players fails to speak in time to the rhythm the game stops, and starts again with this particular person as the new leader	The person who is finding the exercise difficult assumes a more influential position in the group . . .
He begins his own rhythm and then in time to it says, "Who stole the cookie from the cookie jar?" and so on	that allows him to set a slower pace
As the players become proficient the speed of the rhythm can be increased	This will have the effect of intensifying the need to concentrate and react quickly

Variations

---

2. If the players are familiar with the exercise the leader can be a group member.
3. Begin with a very slow and simple rhythm so that the speed of it can be increased later on in the game.
4. Any number from amongst the group members may be used.
5. Or any other number that a group member has.

Word circle (warm-up)

Allow 15–30 minutes

This is an exercise to improve a person's ability to think and speak clearly, especially when he is surprised. It can be used as a *warm-up*.

Recommended for these problems

Model of human occupation	Life-style performance model
Vol. – decreased expectations of success Perf. – difficulty speaking voluntarily due to decrease in spontaneous psychomotor behaviour – difficulty thinking quickly due to deficiencies in process skills – decreased concentration (5 minutes or less)	Sens/mo. – difficulty speaking clearly Cog. – slowness of thought-processing – short attention span Intp. – limited spontaneous conversation

Stage of group development   This is an appropriate exercise for a rather apathetic group of patients who will not or cannot do a physically active exercise.[1]

Synopsis   The exercise takes the form of a non-competitive game, during which a player has to call a predetermined number of words, all beginning with a particular letter of the alphabet. There is a time limit imposed, which is directly proportional to the size of the group and dependent upon an object being passed around the circle from person to person. The ultimate goal of the game is to call out the same number of words as there are people playing.

Materials and equipment   A small object, e.g. book
Small carpeted room.

Procedure

Instruct the players to sit on the floor in as small a circle as possible	This encourages close association with another person and gives a sense of unity to the group

1. This is an excellent game and the authors recommend that it is played frequently as proficiency increases with practice.

Explain the rules of the game as follows:

'The *leader* of this game sits in the centre of the circle while an object is being passed around from player to player at an even speed'

Sitting in the centre of the circle makes the *leader* an integral part of the whole group. Passing the object helps each person to concentrate and remain involved

---

'The *leader* closes his eyes and claps his hands once
He then announces a letter of the alphabet, excluding X and Z'

Two decisions are involved here, when to clap and what letter to call. The *leader* is also required to speak out clearly

---

'When he claps, the person in the group to touch the object last calls out a predetermined number of words[2] beginning with the announced letter'

This encourages fluency in both thinking and speaking. The skills of concentration, retention and recall are used, as well as the ability to select appropriate words. Increased vocabulary may also result

---

The number of words required should be small at first and increased as the players become more proficient

Achieving success in calling the words will improve a person's confidence and decrease his anxiety about failing. This will ultimately enable him to become proficient

---

'Meanwhile the object is still being passed around the circle and if the *caller* fails to list off the required number of words before the object returns to him he replaces the *leader* in the centre of the circle'

This imposes a time limit in which to complete the task and enables the person to experience a situation requiring quick thinking. If a person fails to think of the correct number of words he is not punished, but instead changes his role from that of player to that of leader

---

'If the *caller* succeeds then he remains in his place and the game continues with the original *leader*'[3, 4]

Variations

---

2. The words can be nouns, verbs, adjectives, adverbs, etc.
3. To encourage a sense of responsibility, invite the group as a whole to see that the rules of the game are adhered to. They should also decide on the number of words to be called at any one time (bearing in mind that this number be low enough to provide a sense of achievement and high enough to be challenging).
4. Variations may include: words that rhyme or words in a particular category (e.g. countries, animals).

You really did it this time, Mabel!

Allow 15–30 minutes

This is an exercise in impromptu conversation and interaction.[1] It takes the form of a *theatre game.*[2]

Recommended for these problems

Model of human occupation	Life-style performance model

Vol. – inability to make decisions
     – difficulty initiating conversation due to limited
       interpersonal skills
Perf. – difficulty initiating social interaction
	Cog. – difficulty making choices
	Intp. – limited interpersonal skills
	      – limited ability to initiate conversation

Stage of group development   This exercise is only appropriate for a group that has been together for a while so that members are comfortable with one another and have gained some self-confidence.

Synopsis   Beginning with the words 'You really did it this time, Mabel!' pairs of players take it in turns to enact a conversation in front of the rest of the group.

Materials and equipment   None
Use a familiar quiet room.

Procedure

Invite the players to stand in a circle ...	To facilitate a sense of cohesion and support amongst the members

---

1. This is a difficult exercise and should only be done with adequate preparation with the group in the form of other *theatre games.*
2. The exercise can be *videotaped* and the tape replayed to watch the verbal and nonverbal interaction of the players. The replay can be particularly useful for observing the subtleties of interaction that occur since these will often indicate how a person relates to others during his daily life. These observations can then be used to form the basis for a discussion.

with a *volunteer*[3] in the centre	To give an opportunity for the individual to express his self-confidence and a desire to participate actively

Explain the exercise as follows:
'The player *A* in the centre of the circle is a *neutral person*. That means he is not able to speak until spoken to and will be a partner in any scene that another player wishes to involve him in'

'Player *B*, with a situation in mind approaches *A*, puts his hand on *A*'s shoulder and says "You really did it this time, Mabel!" and follows it up with anything he wishes. For example "You really did it this time, Mabel, you sat on Edna's glasses"'[4]	This requires the ability to create an impromptu situation as well as the desire to initiate a conversation
'*A* then replies in any way that he wishes and the two of them become involved in a dialogue'	To encourage creative thinking and spontaneous verbal interaction The situations used may also necessitate expressing a variety of different ideas and feelings in relation to another person

A conversation develops from the initial exchange, providing the players cooperate with each other. If, however, one of the players consistently negates a statement made by his partner the dialogue will quickly come to an end. For example, 'But Edna is only two years old'

'As the conversation continues any other player *C*[5] may come forward with a different situation'

'He taps *B* on the shoulder in order to interrupt and terminate the dialogue between *A* and *B* and says, "You really did it this time, Mabel ..."'

'*A* leaves and rejoins the circle. *B* replaces *A* as the *neutral person* and *C* becomes *B*. The group is responsible for keeping up the flow of ideas and players involved'[6]	Telling the group this, stimulates them to be actively responsible for the continuation of the exercise

---

3. Demonstrate this exercise, where possible using either staff members (e.g. co-therapist/observer, students) or a fairly verbal group member as the first volunteer.
4. Scenes can be serious, ridiculous, real, fantasy, etc. and the more involved the players become in expressing their ideas and feelings to one another the better.
5. The sense of responsibility for maintaining a conversation or initiating a new one can be quite anxiety-provoking for both staff and patients. It helps to play the game frequently and to keep the dialogue fairly short so that players are involved on centre stage for only brief periods of time.
6. The therapist should be aware when a dialogue is beginning to lose vigour and be prepared to step in with a new situation if volunteers are not coming forward.

After a reasonable period of time the group can be invited to discuss their reactions to the exercise

To provide an opportunity to express feelings related to an experience common to all the participants

Variations

Appendix A: sub-systems of the model of human occupation

The exercises are listed according to the main sub-system which they address in the Model of Human Occupation:

VOLITION

Personal causation   Blind circle (warm-up)
Blind run
Blind walk
Caboose
Comment cards
Expressions
Happiness
How do I appear?
Masks
Now and the future
Painting to music
Self-portrait
Simultaneous conversations
Who am I?

Values   Eavesdropping
Gifts
Personal symbols

Interests   Likes and dislikes

HABITUATION

Roles   Life positions (warm-up)
Support systems
Where am I? (warm-up)

Habits   Hand puppets
Time management

PERFORMANCE

Interpersonal   Feelings
Find the change (warm-up)
Introductions (warm-up)
Mirrors
Nicknames (warm-up)
Pass the ball (warm-up)
People machine (warm-up)

	Story, story
	The chair
	You really did it this time, Mabel!
Process	Balloon debate
	Describe a diagram
	Geography (warm-up)
	Newspaper quiz
	Security
	Soapbox debate
	Story-telling
	Theme collage
Perceptual motor	Action mime (warm-up)
	Building a road (warm-up)
	Kim's game
	Magic box
	Movement and sound circle (warm-up)
	Mystery objects
	Name game (warm-up)
	Playing a sport together
	Rhythm circle (warm-up)
	Salad (warm-up)
	The matchbox is … (warm-up)
	Who stole the cookie? (warm-up)
	Word circle (warm-up)

Appendix B: sub-systems of the life-style performance model

The exercises are listed according to the main sub-system which they address in the Life-style Performance Model:

SENSORY/MOTOR
Building a road (warm-up)
Magic box
Movement and sound circle (warm-up)
Mystery objects
Playing a sport together
Rhythm circle (warm-up)
Salad (warm-up)
The matchbox is ... (warm-up)
Who stole the cookie? (warm-up)

COGNITIVE
Action mime (warm-up)
Balloon debate
Describe a diagram
Geography (warm-up)
Kim's game
Hand puppets
Name game (warm-up)
Newspaper quiz
Now and the future
Security
Soapbox debate
Story, story
Story-telling
Time management
Theme collage
Word circle (warm-up)

PSYCHOLOGICAL
Blind run
Comment cards
Eavesdropping
Expressions
Gifts
Happiness
How do I appear?
Likes and dislikes

Masks
Painting to music
Personal symbols
Self-portrait
Where am I? (warm-up)
Who am I?

INTERPERSONAL   Blind circle (warm-up)
Blind walk
Caboose
Feelings
Find the change (warm-up)
Introductions (warm-up)
Nicknames (warm-up)
Life positions (warm-up)
Mirrors
People machine (warm-up)
Pass the ball (warm-up)
Simultaneous conversations
Support systems
The chair
You really did it this time, Mabel!

Glossary of current psychiatric terms

This includes terms used in this handbook.

Accessible. 'Easy to get along with, talk to, or deal with: capable of being influenced or affected.'[1]

Acting out. 'Expressions of unconscious emotional conflicts or feelings of hostility or love in actions rather than words. The individual is not consciously aware of the meaning of such acts. May be harmful or, in controlled situations, therapeutic (e.g. children's play therapy).'[2]

Activation. 'Stimulation of one organ-system by another; the term stimulation is generally reserved for external influences only.'[3]

Active therapist. 'Type of therapist who makes no effort to remain anonymous but is forceful and expresses his personality definitively in the therapy session.'[4]

Activity. 'In occupational therapy, any occupation or interest wherein participation requires exertion of energy.'[5] See also **Passivity**.

Activity, group. 'In occupational therapy an activity in which several patients participate. Its chief value is its socializing effect upon the mentally ill patients who are asocial.'[6]

Activity, socializing. 'In therapy groups this term denotes the activity that brings an individual into interaction with other members of the group.'[7]

Affect. 'A person's emotional feeling tone and its outward manifestations. Affect and emotion are commonly used interchangeably.'[8]

---

1. *Webster's Third New International Dictionary of the English Language. Unabridged* (1971) p. 11. Springfield: Merriam.
2. Frazier, S. H., Campbell, R. J., Marshall, M. H. & Werner, A. (1975) *A Psychiatric Glossary* p.10. New York: Basic Books.
3. Hinsie, L. E. & Campbell, R. J. (1970) *Psychiatric Dictionary*, 4th edn. p. 12. New York: Oxford University Press.
4. Freedman, A. M., Kaplan, A. I. & Sadock, B. J. (Eds.) (1972) *Modern Synopsis of Psychiatry*, p. 749. Baltimore: Williams & Wilkins.
5. Hinsie & Campbell (1970), p. 13.
6. Ibid. p. 13.
7. Ibid. p. 14.
8. Frazier *et al.*, p. 11.

Affect, blunted. 'A disturbance of affect manifested by dullness of externalized feeling tone. Observed in schizophrenia, it is one of that disorder's fundamental symptoms, according to Eugen Bleuler.'[1]

Aggression. 'A forceful physical, verbal or symbolic action. May be appropriate and self-protective, including healthful self-assertiveness, or inappropriate. Also may be directed outward toward the environment, as in explosive personality, or inward toward the self, as in depression.'[2]

Ambivalence. 'The coexistence of two opposing drives, desires, feelings, or emotions towards the same person, object, or goal. These may be conscious or partly conscious; or one side of the feelings may be unconscious. Example: love and hate toward the same person.'[3]

Anger. 'A strong feeling of displeasure and usually antagonism.'[4]

Anomia. 'Difficulty in recalling the names of things, a variety of **Aphasia**.'[5]

Anxiety. 'Apprehension, tension, or uneasiness that stems from anticipation of danger, the source of which is largely unknown or unrecognized. Primarily of intrapsychic origin, in distinction to fear, which is the emotional response to a consciously recognized and usually external threat or danger.' It 'may be regarded as pathological when present to such an extent as to interfere with effectiveness in living, achievement of desired goals or satisfactions, or reasonable emotional comfort.'[6]

Apathy. Lack of feelings or affect; 'lack of interest and emotional involvement in one's surroundings.'[7]

Aphasia. 'Loss of or impaired ability to speak, write or to understand the meaning of words, due to brain damage.'[8]

Apprehension. When used by psychiatrists, apprehension is almost invariably connected with the feeling of fear, anxiety, or dread. 'There is a tendency, however, to use more circumscribed expressions, such as anxiety, in place of such a general term as apprehension.' The term can also be used to describe 'the intellectual act or process by which a relatively simple object is understood, grasped, or brought before the mind.'[9]

1. Freedman, A. M., Kaplan, A. I. & Sadock, B. J. (Eds.) (1976) *Modern Synopsis of Psychiatry/II, 2nd edn.*, p. 1280. Baltimore: Williams & Wilkins.
2. Frazier *et al.*, p. 11.
3. Ibid. p. 13.
4. Webster (1971), p. 82.
5. Drever, James (1965) A Dictionary of Psychology, p. 16. Harmondsworth: Penguin.
6. Frazier *et al.*, p. 16.
7. Freedman *et al.* (1972), p. 753.
8. Wolman, p. 29.
9. Hinsie & Campbell (1970), pp. 59/60.

Appropriate. 'Specially suitable.'[1]

Asocial. 'Not social; indifferent to social values; without social meaning or significance.'[2]

Assertive. 'Characterized by self-confidence, determination, and boldness in asserting opinions or in otherwise making one's presence or influence felt.'[3] See also **Self-assertion**.

Assessment. 'The act of assessing: an evaluation.'[4]

Assess, to. 'To analyse critically and judge definitively the nature, significance, status or merit of.'[5]

Attention and concentration. 'The aspect of consciousness that relates to the amount of effort exerted in focusing on certain aspects of an experience.'[6]

Attitude. The 'preparatory mental posture with which one receives stimuli and reacts to them.'[7]

Awareness. 'Mere experience of an object or idea; sometimes equivalent to consciousness.'[8]

Behaviour. 'The manner in which anything acts or operates. With regard to the human being the term usually refers to the action of the individual as a unit. He may be, and ordinarily is, acting in response to some given organ or impulse, but it is his general reaction that gives rise to the concept of behaviour.'[9]

Body awareness. See **Body image**.

Body image. The conscious and unconscious picture a person has of his own body at any moment. The conscious and unconscious images may differ from each other.

Body language. 'The system by which a person expresses his thoughts and feelings by means of his bodily activity.'[10]

Closed system. 'A system which does not interact with its environment or exhibit properties of life.'[11]

Cognitive functions. 'Referring to the mental process of comprehension, judgement, memory, and reasoning, as contrasted with emotional and volitional processes. Contrast with **Conative**.'[12]

---

1. Webster (1971), p. 66.
2. Hinsie & Campbell (1970), p. 66.
3. Webster (1971), p. 131.
4. Ibid.
5. Ibid.
6. Freedman *et al.*, (1972), p. 754.
7. Ibid.
8. Drever, p. 26
9. Hinsie & Campbell (1970), p. 90.
10. Freedman *et al.*, (1976), p. 1286.
11. Kielhofner, G. (Ed.) (1985) *A Model of Human Occupation, Theory and Application*. Baltimore: Williams & Wilkins.
12. Frazier *et al.*, p. 33.

Communication. The 'transmission of emotions, attitudes, ideas, and acts from one person to another. The distinction is made between the "primary" techniques of communication common to all men, such as language, gesture, the imitation of overt behaviour and social suggestion, and the "secondary" techniques which facilitate communication, such as writing, symbolic systems including stop-and-go lights, bugle-calls and other signals, and physical conditions allowing for communication such as the telephone, railroad and the airplane.'[1]

Communication/interaction skills. 'Abilities for sharing and receiving information and for coordinating one's behaviour with that of others in order to accomplish mutual activities and goals.'[2]

Communication, nonverbal. See **Nonverbal interaction**.

Communication, verbal. See **Verbalization** or **Verbal technique**.

Competence. 'The quality of being able or having the capacity to respond effectively to the demands of one or a range of situations,'[3]

Comprehension. 'Understanding, especially as opposed to mere apprehending or cognition.'[4]

Conative. 'Pertains to the basic strivings of an individual as expressed in his behaviour and actions; volitional as contrasted with cognitive.'[5]

Concentration. See **Attention**.

Conflict. 'A mental struggle that arises from the simultaneous operation of opposing impulses, drives, or external (environmental) or internal drives; termed intrapsychic when the conflict is between forces within the personality; extrapsychic when it is between the self and the environment.'[6]

Confrontation. 'Act of letting a person know where one stands in relationship to him, what one is experiencing, and how one perceives him.'[7]

Confusion. 'Disturbed orientation in respect of time, place, or person'[8] See **Mental status**.

Conscious. 'That part of the mind or mental functioning of which the content is subject to awareness or known to the person. In neurology: awake, alert. Contrast with unconscious.'[9]

Contraindication. 'A reason for not doing something; more specifically, a feature or complication of a condition that countermands the use of a therapeutic agent that might otherwise be applied.'[10]

---

1. Hinsie, L. E. & Campbell, R. J. (1960) *Psychiatric Dictionary*, 3rd edn., p. 135. New York: Oxford University Press.
2. Kielhofner *et al.*, (1985), p. 502.
3. Kielhofner *et al.*, (1985), p. 502.
4. Hinsie & Campbell, (1970), p. 147.
5. Frazier *et al.*, p. 35.
6. Ibid., p. 36.
7. Freedman *et al.*, (1972), p. 756.
8. Frazier *et al.*, p. 36.
9. Ibid.
10. Hinsie & Campbell (1970), p. 161.

Conversation. 'Oral exchange of sentiments, observations, opinions, ideas: colloquial discourse.'[1]

Cooperation: 'To act or work together with another or others for a common purpose; a joint effort or operation.'[2]

Coordination. 'Harmonious action, as of muscles.'[3]

Creativity. The 'ability to produce something new. Silvano Arieti describes creativity as the tertiary process, a balanced continuation of primary and secondary processes, whereby materials from the id are used in the service of the ego.'[4]

Debility. 'Weakness.'[5]

Decision. 'The act of making up one's mind; the act of forming an opinion or deciding upon a course of action; a judgement or conclusion reached or given.'[6]

Defence mechanism. 'Unconscious intrapsychic processes serving to provide relief from emotional conflict and anxiety. Conscious efforts are frequently made for the same reasons, but true defence mechanisms are unconscious. Some common defence mechanisms are: compensation, conversion, denial, displacement, dissociation, idealization, identification, incorporation, introjection, projection, rationalization, reaction formation, regression, sublimation, substitution, symbolization, undoing.'[7] See **Mental mechanism**.

Delusion. 'A firm, fixed idea not amenable to rational explanation. Maintained against logical argument despite objective contradictory evidence. Common delusions include:

> *delusions of grandeur*: exaggerated ideas of one's importance or identity.
>
> *delusions of persecution*: ideas that one has been singled out for persecution. See also **Paranoia**.
>
> *delusions of reference*: incorrect assumption that certain casual or unrelated events or the behaviour of others apply to oneself.'[8]

Dependency. 'This generally means "a form of behaviour which suggests inability to make decisions; marked inclination to lean on others for advice, guidance, support, etc." (Hamilton, G. (1930) *A Medical Social Terminology*. New York: Presbyterian Hospital.'[9]

Depression. In psychiatry, a morbid state characterized by a marked sadness, low self-esteem and self-reproach, psychomotor retardation, withdrawal and at times by the desire to die. It should be differentiated from grief which is realistic and proportionate to what has been lost. Depression may be a symptom of any psychiatric disorder or may constitute its principal manifestation.

---

1. Webster (1971), p. 498.
2. Webster (1968), p. 325.
3. Faber, p. 106
4. Freedman *et al.*, (1972), p. 761.
5. Faber, p. 118.
6. Webster (1968), p. 380.
7. Frazier *et al.*, p. 40.
8. Ibid., p. 41.
9. Hinsie & Campbell (1970), p. 199.

Dialogue. 'A conversation between two or more persons.'[1] Compare with **Monologue**.

Disappointment. 'The state or condition of being disappointed: failure of expectation or hope.'[2]

Discuss, to. 'To examine, to talk about; take up in conversation or in a discourse; consider and argue the pros and cons of.
> *Syn*: to discuss implies talking about something in a deliberate fashion, with varying opinions offered constructively and usually amicably.'[3]

Discussion. 'Consideration of a question in open, usually informal, debate.'[4]

Distractibility. 'Inability to focus one's attention.'[5]

Dominance. In psychiatry, 'an individual's disposition to play a prominent or controlling role in his interaction with others.'[6]

Ego. 'In psychoanalytic theory ... the ego represents the sum of certain mental mechanisms, such as perception and memory, and specific defence mechanisms. The ego serves to mediate between the demands of primitive instinctual drives (the id), of internalized parental and social prohibitions (the superego), and of reality. The compromises between these forces achieved by the ego tend to resolve intrapsychic conflict and serve as an adaptive and executive function.'[7]

Ego boundary. 'A concept introduced by *Federn* to refer to "the peripheral sense organ of the ego." The ego boundary discriminates what is real from what is unreal. There are two main ego boundaries, the inner and the outer.'[8] The inner boundary prevents the entrance of repressed material into the conscious, while the outer one is the boundary toward stimuli of the external world.

Egocentric. 'Refers to a person who is self-centred, preoccupied with his own needs, selfish and lacking interest in others.'[9]

Ego-strength. 'The effectiveness with which the ego discharges its various functions. A strong ego will not only mediate between id, superego, and reality and integrate these functions, but further it will do so with enough flexibility so that energy will remain for re-activity and other needs. This is in contrast to the rigid personality in which ego functions are maintained, but only at the cost of impoverishment of the personality.'[10]

Emotion. 'A feeling such as fear, anger, grief, joy or love which may not always be conscious.'[11] See also **Affect** and **Feeling**.

---

1. Webster (1971), p. 622.
2. Ibid., p. 643.
3. Webster (1968), p. 418.
4. Webster (1971), p. 648.
5. Freedman *et al.*, (1972), p. 763.
6. Frazier *et al.*, p. 45.
7. Ibid., p. 48.
8. Hinsie & Campbell (1960), p. 101.
9. Freedman *et al.*, (1972) p. 765.
10. Hinsie & Campbell (1970) p. 256.
11. Frazier *et al.*, p. 50.

Empathy. 'An objective and insightful awareness of the feelings, emotions, and behaviour of another person, their meaning and significance; usually subjective and noncritical. Contrast with **Sympathy**.'[1]

Environment. 'The objects, persons and events with which a system interacts.'[2]

Evaluate. 'To examine and judge concerning the worth, quality, significance, amount, degree or condition of.'[3]

Evaluation. 'The act or result of evaluating.'[4] See **Assessment**.

Exercise. 'Repetition of an act in order to learn it or increase skill.'[5]

Expectations of Success or Failure. 'One's anticipation of future endeavours and whether their outcomes will be successful or not.'[6]

Experiencing. 'Feeling emotions and feelings as opposed to thinking; being involved in what is happening, rather than standing back at a distance and theorizing.'[7]

Extemporaneous. 'Impromptu; performed on the spur of the moment.'[8]

External and Internal Locus of Control. 'The individual's conviction that outcomes in life are related to personal actions (internal control) versus the action of others, fate or luck (external control).'[9]

Extraversion. 'A state in which attention and energies are largely directed outward from the self.'[10] Contrast with **Introversion**.

Eye-contact. Describes the mutual glances that occur between people during social interaction. The degree of eye-contact depends on such factors as whether the participants like one another, how involved they are in their discussion, the nature of the topic under discussion and their physical position in relation to one another. The degree of eye-contact may also follow a cultural pattern that presumes touching, no touch, interpersonal spacing and the way people orient their bodies.

Feedback. 'The process of returning to the system information concerning output and its consequences.'[11] Communication to the sender of the effect his original message had on those to whom it was relayed. Feedback may alter or re-enforce the original idea; it is a function that is basic to correction and self-correction.'[12]

Feeling. '(1) Subjective description for awareness of bodily (neutral) states that cannot be reliably referred to environmental wants.

---

1. Ibid., p. 51.
2. Kielhofner *et al.*, (1985), p. 503.
3. Webster (1971), p. 786.
4. Ibid.
5. Wolman, Benjamin 1. (1973) *Dictionary of Behavioural Science* p. 131. New York: Litton Educational Publishing.
6. Kielhofner *et al.* (1985), p. 17.
7. Freedman *et al.* (1976), p. 1300.
8. Webster (1971), p. 804.
9. Kielhofner *et al.*, (1985), p. 16.
10. Frazier *et al.*, p. 54.
11. Kielhofner *et al.*, (1985), p. 503.
12. Hinsie & Campbell (1970), p. 298.

(2) Tactile sensation. (3) Awareness of something, i.e. feeling of being accepted. (4) Emotion, e.g. feeling happy, sad, angry, etc.'[1]

Flight of ideas. 'Verbal skipping from one idea to another. The ideas appear to be continuous but are fragmentary and determined by chance or temporal associations. Sometimes seen in manic-depressive psychosis.'[2]

Focus. 'A central point: a point of concentration or of emanation: to cause to be concentrated.'[3]

Gesture. This refers to any action or posture intended to express an idea or feeling or to enforce or emphasize an argument, assertion or opinion. It is a form of nonverbal communication using the hands and to a lesser extent the head and feet.

Goal. 'In sociology ... the term goal denotes any change in a situation which a person or group intends to bring about through his or its action.'[4] Synonyms of goal are end, objective and purpose.

Group. 'A number of objects or individuals capable of being regarded as a collective unit, or having a unity of its own; a pattern or configuration of objects perceived as a whole or Gestalt.'[5]

Group cohesion. 'Effect of the mutual bonds between members of a group as a result of their concentrated effort for a common interest and purpose. Until cohesiveness is achieved, the group cannot concentrate its full energy on a common task.'[6]

Group dynamics. This 'denotes the study of (a) the structure and functioning of groups, notably the psychological aspects of "small groups", with especial reference to the changing pattern of intra-group adjustment, tension, conflict and cohesion; and (b) the shifts in relationships of one group with another.'[7]

Group pressure. 'Demand by group member that individual members submit and conform to group standards, values and behaviour.'[8]

Habit organization. 'The degree to which one has a typical use of time which supports competent performance in a variety of environments and roles and provides a balance of activity.'[9]

Habits. 'Images guiding the routine and typical ways in which a person performs.'[10]

Habituation subsystem. 'A collection of images which trigger and guide the performance of routine patterns of behaviour.'[11]

Hallucination. 'A false sensory perception in the absence of an actual

---

1. Wolman, p. 143.
2. Frazier *et al.*, p. 56.
3. Webster (1971), p. 881.
4. Gould, J & Kolb, W. L. (Eds.) (1964) *A Dictionary of the Social Sciences*, p. 290. London: Tavistock.
5. Drever, p. 112.
6. Freedman, *et al.*, (1972), p. 770.
7. Gould & Kolb, p. 297.
8. Freedman, *et al.*, (1972), p. 770.
9. Kielhofner *et al.*, (1985), p. 504.
10. Kielhofner *et al.*, (1985), p. 504.
11. Kielhofner *et al.*, (1985), p. 504.

external stimulus. May be induced by emotional and other factors, such as drugs, alcohol and stress. May occur in any of the senses.'[1]

Honesty. 'In therapy, honesty is a value manifested by the ability to communicate one's immediate experience, including inconsistent, conflicting or ambivalent feelings and perceptions.'[2]

Hyperactive. 'Excessively or abnormally active.'[3]

Id. 'In Freudian theory, that part of the personality structure which harbours the unconscious instinctual desires and strivings of the individual.'[4] See **Ego** and **Superego**.

Identity-crises. 'A loss of the sense of sameness and historical continuity of one's self, an inability to accept or adopt the role the subject perceives as being expected of him by society; often expressed by isolation, withdrawal, extremism, rebelliousness, and negativity, and typically triggered by a combination of sudden increases in the strength of instinctual drives in a milieu of rapid social evolution and technological change.'[5]

Improvisation. 'In psychodrama, the acting out of problems without prior preparation;'[6] to perform or act on the spur of the moment without any preparation.

Impulse. 'A psychic striving; usually refers to an instinctual urge.'[7]

Inadequate. 'Lacking the capacity for psychological maturity; unable to make adequate social adjustment.'[8]

Indecision. 'Inability or failure to arrive at a decision; wavering between two or more courses of action.'[9]

Individual. 'Jung defines the psychological individual as a "unique being". The psychological individual is characterized by its peculiar, and in certain respects, unique psychology.'[10]

Individuation. 'The process of forming and specializing the individual nature; in particular, it is the development of the psychological individual as a differentiated being from the general, collective psychology.'[11]

Inhibition. 'In psychiatry, an unconscious defence against forbidden instinctual drives; it may interfere with or restrict specific activities or general patterns of behaviour.'[12]

Initiation. 'The process of beginning an activity or movement.'[13]

Insight. 'Self-understanding. The extent of the individual's understanding of the origin, nature, and mechanisms of his attitudes and

1. Frazier *et al.*, p. 61.
2. Freedman *et al.*, (1972), p. 771.
3. Faber, p. 213.
4. Frazier *et al.*, p.64.
5. Ibid., p. 65.
6. Freedman *et al.*, (1976), p. 1308.
7. Frazier *et al.*, p. 66.
8. Webster (1971), p. 1139.
9. Ibid., p. 1146.
10. Hinsie & Campbell (1970), p. 390.
11. Hinsie & Campbell (1970), p. 390.
12. Sternberg, R. J. (1982), *Handbook of Human Intelligence*, pp. 600–601. Cambridge: Cambridge University Press.
13. Drever, p. 138.

behaviour. More superficially, recognition by a patient that he is ill.'[1] 'Most therapists distinguish two types: (1) intellectual insight: knowledge and awareness without any change of maladaptive behaviour; (2) emotional or visceral insight: awareness, knowledge, and understanding of one's own maladaptive behaviour, leading to positive changes in personality and behaviour.'[2]

Intake. 'The importation of energy and information from the environment.'[3]

Intelligence. 'According to Thorndike, there are three distinct types of intelligence; abstract, mechanical and social. The capacity to understand and manage abstract ideas and symbols constitutes abstract intelligence; the ability to understand, invent and manage mechanisms comprises mechanical intelligence; and the capacity to act reasonably and wisely as regards human relations and social affairs constitutes social intelligence.'[4]

Intelligence quotient. 'The score obtained from one of various intelligence tests. This score is calculated for an individual in comparison with the so-called average or normal intelligence for his age. The tests measure 'abstracting ability, reasoning, speed of visual information processing and many other formal cognitive processes.' Aside from this cognitive factor, the I.Q. score is also influenced by motivation and achievement factors.'[5]

Inter- (Lat.) 'Prefix meaning "between" or "among".'[6]

Interact. 'To act on each other; act reciprocally.'[7]

Interaction. See **Social interaction** and **Nonverbal interaction**.

Interests. Dispositions to find occupations pleasurable.[8]

Interpersonal relations. 'Refers to everything that occurs between one person and another (or others) by way of perception, evaluation, understanding and mode of reaction.'[9]

Interpersonal skill. 'Ability of a person in relationship with others to express his feelings appropriately, to be socially responsive, to change and influence, and to work and create.'[10] See **Socialization**.

Intra- (Lat.) 'Prefix meaning "within" or "inside".'[11]

Intrapsychic. See **Conflict**.

Introversion. 'Preoccupation with oneself and accompanying reduction of interest in the outside world; the reverse of extraversion.'[12]

Isolation. 'A defence mechanism, operating unconsciously, in which an unacceptable impulse, idea, or act is separated from its original memory source, thereby removing the emotional charge

---

1. Frazier, *et al.*, p. 89.
2. Freedman *et al.*, (1976), p. 1309.
3. Kielhofner *et al.*, (1985), p. 504.
4. Hinsie & Campbell, (1970), p. 406.
5. Ibid., p. 640.
6. Webster (1968), p. 761.
7. Ibid.
8. Kielhofner *et al.*, (1985), p. 504.
9. Gould & Kolb, p. 350.
10. Freedman *et al.*, (1976), p. 1310.
11. Drever, p. 144.
12. Frazier *et al.*, p. 90.

associated with the original memory.'[1] 'Isolation may (also) be defined as a lack of family and social contacts' and as such it 'has to be distinguished from loneliness, although the two often co-exist.'[2]

Judgement. 'Mental act of comparing or evaluating choices within the framework of a given set of values for the purpose of selecting a course of action. Judgement is said to be intact if the course of action chosen is consistent with reality. Judgement is said to be impaired if the chosen course of action is not consistent with reality.'[3]

Kinesics (kinesiology). 'The study of body movement as part of the process of communication; sociological analysis of interactional activity.'[4] Kinesics includes the study of body posture, movement and facial expression.

Labile. 'Unstable, characterized by rapidly changing emotions.'[5]
Leadership. 'Leadership "may be broadly defined as the relation between an individual and a group built around some common interest and behaving in a manner directed or determined by him." (Schmidt, R. (1933) *Leadership*; *Encyclopaedia of the Social Sciences*, Vol. 9, p. 282. New York: Macmillan).'[6]
Leadership role. 'Stance adopted by the therapist in conducting a group. There are three main leadership roles: authoritarian, democratic, and laissez-faire. Any group — social, therapeutic, training or task-oriented — is primarily influenced by the role practised by the leader.'[7]

Mania. 'A mood disorder characterized by excessive elation, hyperactivity, agitation, and accelerated thinking and speaking, sometimes manifested in a flight of ideas. Mania is seen most frequently as one of the two major forms of manic-depression psychosis.'[8]
Manic-depression psychosis. 'A major affective disorder characterized by severe mood swings and a tendency to remission and recurrence.'[9] See also **Depression**.
Medium, media. 'A condition, atmosphere, or environment in which something may function or flourish: the material or technical means for artistic expression (as paint, canvas ... or musical form).'[10]

1. Frazier et al., p. 90.
2. Leigh, D., Pare, C. M. B. & Marks, J. (Eds.) (1977) *A Concise Encyclopaedia of Psychiatry*, p. 207. Baltimore: University Park Press.
3. Freedman *et al.* (1976), p. 1311.
4. Frazier *et al.*, p. 92.
5. Freedman *et al.*, (1976), p. 1312.
6. Hinsie & Campbell (1970), p. 429.
7. Freedman *et al.*, (1972), p. 777.
8. Frazier *et al.*, p. 97.
9. Ibid., p. 90.
10. Webster (1971), p. 1403.

Memory. 'Ability to revive past sensory impressions, experiences and learned ideas. Memory includes three basic mental processes:

  registration: the ability to perceive, recognize and establish information in the central nervous system;

  retention: the ability to retain registered information; and

  recall: the ability to retrieve stored information at will.'[1]

Mental disorder. 'Any psychiatric illness or disease included in the World Health Organization's *International Classification of Diseases*.'[2]

Mental mechanism. 'A generic term for a variety of psychic processes that are functions of the ego and largely unconscious. Includes perception, memory, thinking and defence mechanisms.'[3]

Mental status. 'The level and style of functioning of the psyche, used in its broadest sense to include intellectual functioning as well as the emotional, attitudinal, psychological and personality aspects of the subject; in clinical psychiatry, the term is commonly used to refer to the results of the examination of the patient's mental state. Such an examination ordinarily aims to achieve one or more of the following:

(1) evaluation and assessment of any psychiatric condition present, including provisional diagnosis and prognosis, determination of degree of impairment, suitability for treatment, and indications for particular types of therapeutic intervention.

(2) formulation of the personality structure of the subject, which may suggest the historical and developmental antecedents of whatever psychiatric condition exists;

(3) estimate of the ability and willingness of the subject to participate appropriately in the treatment regimen considered desirable for him. The mental status is reported in a series of narrative statements describing such things as: affect, speech, thought content, perceptions, and cognitive functions, including orientation.'[4]

Mime. 'The art of creating and portraying a character or of narration by body movement (as by realistic and symbolic gestures); (to) play a part with mimic gesture and action usually without words.'[5]

Monologue. 'A long speech uttered by one person while in company with others.'[6] Contrast with **Dialogue**.

Mood. The 'feeling tone that is experienced by a person internally. Mood does not include the external expression of the internal feeling tone.'[7] See also **Affect**.

Motivation. The 'force that pushes a person to act to satisfy a need. It implies an incentive or desire that influences the will and causes the person to act.'[8]

---

1. Freedman *et al.*, (1972), p. 779.
2. Frazier *et al.*, p. 99.
3. Ibid.
4. Frazier *et al.*, p.100.
5. Webster(1971), p. 1436.
6. Ibid., p. 1463.
7. Freedman *et al.*, (1976), p. 1316.
8. Freedman et al., p. 1317.

Negative feelings. In psychiatry these refer to unfriendly or hostile feelings.

Neologism. 'Neologisms are part of the speech disturbance which reflects the disordered thoughts of schizophrenics. They are words of the patient's own making, often condensations of other words and having a special meaning for the patient.'[1]

Neurosis (psychoneurosis). 'An emotional maladaptation arising from an unresolved unconscious conflict. The anxiety is either felt directly or modified by various psychological mechanisms to produce other, subjectively distressing symptoms. The neuroses are usually considered less severe than the psychoses (although not always less disabling) because they manifest neither gross personality disorganization nor gross distortion or misinterpretation of external reality. The neuroses are classified according to predominating symptoms. The common neuroses are: anxiety neurosis, depersonalization neurosis, depressive neurosis, hypochondriacal neurosis, hysterical neurosis (a) conversion type, or (b) dissociative type, neurasthenic neurosis, obsessive compulsive neurosis, phobic neurosis.'[2]

Nonverbal interaction. Technique used without the aid of words in groups to promote communication and intimacy and to bypass verbal defences. Many exercises of this sort are carried out in complete silence; in others the participants emit grunts, groans, yells, cries or sighs. Gestalt therapy pays particular attention to nonverbal expression.

Objective. 'Expressing or involving the use of facts without distortion by personal feelings or prejudices.'[3]

Observation. 'An act of recognizing and noting some fact or occurrence.'[4]

Obsessive-compulsive (psycho) neurosis. 'A type of psychoneurosis characterized by disturbing, unwanted, anxiety-provoking, intruding thoughts or ideas, and repetitive impulses to perform acts (ceremonials, counting, hand-washing, etc.) which may be considered abnormal, undesirable or distasteful to the patient.'[5]

Open system. 'A composition of interrelated structures and functions organized into a coherent whole that interacts with an environment and that is capable of maintaining and changing itself.'[6]

Opinion. 'A belief not based on absolute certainty or positive knowledge but on what seems true, valid or probable to one's own mind.'[7]

Optimum. 'The amount or degree of something that is most favourable to some end.'[8]

---

1. Leigh *et al.*, p. 254.
2. Frazier *et al.*, p. 106.
3. Webster (1971), p. 1556.
4. Ibid., p. 1558.
5. Hinsie & Campbell (1970), p. 519.
6. Kielhofner *et al.*, (1985), p. 506.
7. Webster (1968) p. 1028.
8. Ibid. (1971) p. 1585.

Orientation. 'Awareness of one's self in relation to time, place and person.'[1]

Output. 'The action of the system directed at the environment.'[2]

Overinclusion. 'Overinclusive thinking is one aspect of thought disorder in acute schizophrenia. There is an inability to preserve conceptual boundaries, so that ideas only distinctly related to a particular concept become included in that concept. The "wooliness" of schizophrenic thought is a result of this type of thought disorder.'[3]

Paranoid. 'An adjective applied to individuals who are overly suspicious.'[4]

Parkinsonism. See **Tremor**.

Participation. 'The action or state of taking part with others in an activity.'[5] See also **Activity**.

Passivity. 'One of the several modalities of adaptation. For example, it is possible for the organism to adapt itself to its environment by going either forward to meet it or backward to escape it. The first procedure would be termed the modality of activity in adaptive behaviour, while the latter would be termed the modality of passivity.'[6]

Patient. 'A sick person.'[7]

Perception. 'Mental processes by which data — intellectual, sensory and emotional — are organized meaningfully. Through perception a person makes sense out of the many stimuli that bombard him. It is one of the many ego functions.'[8]

Perceptual expansion. 'Development of one's ability to recognize and interpret the meaning of sensory stimuli through associations with past experiences with similar stimuli. Perceptual expansion through the relaxation of defences is one of the goals of both individual and group therapy.'[9]

Perceptual motor skills. 'Abilities for interpreting sensory information and for manipulating self and objects.'[10]

Performance subsystem. 'A collection of images and biological structures and processes which are organized into skills and used in the production of purposeful behaviour.'[11]

Personal causation. 'A collection of beliefs and expectations which a person holds about his or her effectiveness in the environment.'[12]

---

1. Frazier *et al.*, p. 111.
2. Kielhofner *et al.* (1985), p. 506.
3. Leigh *et al.*, p.268.
4. Frazier *et al.*, p. 112.
5. Webster (1971), p. 1646.
6. Hinsie & Campbell (1970), p. 548.
7. Faber, p. 337.
8. Freedman *et al.*, (1976), p. 1320.
9. Ibid.
10. Kielhofner *et al.*, (1985), p. 507.
11. Kielhofner *et al.*, (1985), p. 507.
12. Kielhofner *et al.*, (1985), p. 507.

Personality. 'The characteristic way in which a person behaves; the ingrained pattern of behaviour that each person evolves, both consciously and unconsciously, as his style of life or way of being in adapting to his environment,'[1] See **Personality disorders**.

Personality disorders. 'A group of mental disorders characterized by deeply ingrained maladaptive patterns of behaviour, generally life-long in duration and consequently often recognizable by the time of adolescence or earlier. Affecting primarily the personality of the individual they are different in quality from neurosis and psychosis.'[2]

Philosophy. 'A critical examination of the grounds for fundamental beliefs and an analysis of the basic concepts employed in the expression of such beliefs.'[3]

Positive feelings. In psychiatry these refer to warm, friendly feelings as opposed to negative hostile feelings.

Poverty of ideas. Identified as a lack of spontaneous thoughts, ideas and associations. It is a psychiatric term describing a form of thought disorder often seen in schizophrenia.

Problem. 'An unsettled matter demanding solution or decision and requiring ... considerable thought or skill for its proper solution or decision: something that is a source of perplexity or worry.'[4]

Process skills. 'Abilities directed at managing events or processes in the environment.'[5]

Projection. 'Unconscious defence mechanism in which a person attributes to another the ideas, thoughts, feelings, and impulses that are part of his inner perceptions but that are unacceptable to him. Projection protects the person from anxiety arising from an inner conflict. By externalizing whatever is unacceptable, the person deals with it as a situation apart from himself.'[6]

Projective techniques. 'Methods used to discover an individual's attitudes, motivations, defensive manoeuvres and characteristic ways of responding through analysis of their responses to un-structured, ambiguous stimuli.'[7] As a group treatment procedure they may make use of the spontaneous creative work of each patient. For example, group members make and analyse drawings, which in turn often express their underlying emotional problems.

Psychiatry. 'The medical science that deals with the origin, diagnosis, prevention and treatment of mental disorders.'[8]

Psychological functions. Skill and performance in developing one's self-concept and self-identity.

Psychomotor. 'Relating to voluntary movement.'[9]

---

1. Frazier *et al.*, p. 115.
2. Ibid., p. 116.
3. Webster (1971), p. 1698.
4. Ibid., p. 1807.
5. Kielhofner *et al.*, (1985), p. 508.
6. Freedman *et al.*, (1976), p. 1322.
7. Wolman, p. 291.
8. Frazier *et al.*, p. 124.
9. Faber, p. 368.

Psychomotor retardation. 'A generalized "retardation" of physical and emotional reactions.'[1]

Psychosis. 'A major mental disorder of organic or emotional origin in which the individual's ability to think, respond emotionally, remember, communicate, interpret reality, and behave appropriately is sufficiently impaired so as to interfere grossly with his capacity to meet the ordinary demands of life. Often characterized by regressive behaviour, inappropriate mood, diminished impulse control, and such abnormal mental content as delusions and hallucinations. The term is applicable to conditions having a wide range of severity and duration.'[2] See **Schizophrenia**, **Manic-depressive psychosis**, **Depression** and **Reality testing**.

Purpose. See **Goal**.

Reaction(s). 'Counter-action; response to a stimulus.'[3]

Reality. 'The totality of objective things and factual events. Reality includes everything that is perceived by a person's special senses and is validated by other people.'[4]

Reality, control with. See **Reality testing**.

Reality testing. A 'fundamental ego function that consists of objective evaluation and judgement of the world outside the self. By interacting with his animate and inanimate environment, a person tests its real nature, as well as his own relation to it. How the person evaluates reality and his attitudes towards it are determined by early experiences with significant persons in his life.'[5] 'The ability to evaluate the external world objectively and differentiate adequately between it and the internal world, between self and non-self. Falsification of reality, as with massive denial or projection, indicates a severe disturbance of ego functioning and/or the perceptual and memory processes upon which it is partly based.'[6] See also **Ego** and **Psychosis**.

Reasoning. 'A process of thinking involving inference, or of solving problems by employing general principles.'[7]

Recall. 'The process of bringing memory into consciousness.' In psychiatry, 'recall is often used to refer to the recollection of facts and events in the immediate past.'[8] See **Memory**.

Recognition. 'Perceiving (or recalling) an object, accompanied by a feeling of familiarity, or the conviction that the same object has been perceived before.'[9] 'To acknowledge as worthy of appreciation or approval.'[10]

---

1. Frazier *et al.*, p. 126.
2. Frazier *et al.*, p. 127.
3. Hinsie & Campbell (1970), p. 645.
4. Freedman et al., (1976), p. 1325.
5. Ibid.
6. Frazier *et al.*, p. 131.
7. Drever, p. 241.
8. Frazier *et al.*, p. 131.
9. Drever, p. 242.
10. Webster (1968), p. 1214.

Relatedness. 'The interrelation between two or more people who reciprocally influence each other, as patient-therapist, mother-child, etc. Normal relatedness is based on security in interpersonal relations and in large part is a result of early childhood experiences.'[1]

Relatedness, functional. 'The arrangement of objects that are organically and dynamically related to each other; for example, placing woodworking tools near the woodworking bench and nails and other objects involved in woodworking nearby; placing drawing paper near crayons and paints in the proximity of an easel.'[2]

Relaxation. 'Diminution of tension.'[3]

Repression. 'A defence mechanism, operating unconsciously, that banishes unacceptable ideas, affects or impulses from consciousness, or that keeps out of consciousness what has never been conscious. Although not subject to voluntary recall, the repressed material may emerge in disguised form. Often confused with the conscious mechanism of suppression.'[4]

Resistance. 'The individual's conscious or unconscious psychological defence against bringing repressed (unconscious) thoughts to light.'[5] See **Mental mechanism**.

Retardation. 'Slowness or backwardness of intellectual development; when used in this sense, mental retardation is the usual phrase. Slowness of response, a slowing down of thinking and/or a decrease in psychomotor activity; in this latter sense, the term psychomotor retardation is the appropriate phrase. Psychomotor retardation is characteristic of clinical depressions.'[6]

Risk. 'The chance of incurring damage or a loss of some kind (physical, psychological, military, political, economic, etc.).'[7] In psychiatry the term is usually used to mean 'taking a chance' or 'exposing oneself to the chance of . . .'.

Role. 'Pattern of behaviour that a person takes. It has its roots in childhood and is influenced by significant people with whom the person has primary relationships. When the behaviour pattern conforms with the expectations and demands of other people, it is said to be a complementary role. If it does not conform with the demands and expectations of others, it is known as a non-complementary role.'[8]

Role balance. Integration of an optimal number of appropriate roles into one's life.[9]

---

1. Hinsie & Campbell (1970), p. 658.
2. Ibid.
3. Faber, p. 379.
4. Frazier *et al.*, p. 133.
5. Ibid.
6. Hinsie & Campbell (1970), p. 665.
7. Gould & Kolb, p. 605.
8. Freedman et al., (1976), p. 1327.
9. Kielhofner et al., (1985), p. 508.

Role-playing. 'Psychodrama technique in which a person is trained to function more effectively in his reality roles, such as employer, employee, student or instructor.'[1]

Schizophrenia. 'A large group of disorders, usually of psychotic proportion, manifested by characteristic disturbances of thought, mood and behaviour. Thought disturbances are marked by alterations of concept formation that may lead to misinterpretation of reality and sometimes to delusions and hallucinations. Mood changes include ambivalence, constriction, inappropriateness, and loss of empathy with others. Behaviour may be withdrawn, regressive, and bizarre.'[2]

Sedentary. '(1) Used in sitting. (2) Related to the habit of sitting.'[3]

Self-analysis. 'Investigation of one's own psychic components.'[4]

Self-assertion. 'The act of demanding recognition for oneself or of asserting or insisting upon one's rights, claims, etc.'[5]

Self-awareness. 'Sense of knowing what one is experiencing; for example, realizing that one has responded with anger to another group member as a substitute for the anxiety left when he attacked a vital part of one's self-concept. Self-awareness is a major goal of all therapy, individual or group.'[6]

Self-conception. An individual's self-conception is his view of himself. Self-conception is the equivalent to the self, if the latter is defined as 'the individual as perceived by that individual in a socially determined form of reference.' In addition to a view of self, self-conception includes notions of one's interests and aversions, a conception of one's goals and success in achieving them, a picture of the ideological frame of reference through which one views oneself and other objects and some knowledge of self-evaluation.

Self-confidence. 'The quality of being self-confident; belief in or reliance on oneself or one's abilities.'[7]

Self-consciousness. 'Awareness of one's own existence, thoughts and actions; popularly, embarrassment or shyness.'[8]

Self-esteem. 'Belief in one-self; self-respect.'[9] 'A state of being on good terms with one's superego. Pathological loss of self-esteem is characteristic of clinical depression.'[10]

Self-expression. 'The expression of one's own personality or emotions, especially through some art form.'[11]

Self-respect. 'A proper respect for oneself, one's character and one's behaviour.'[12] See **Self-esteem**.

---

1. Freedman *et al.*, (1976), p. 1327.
2. Frazier et al., p. 134.
3. Faber, p. 396.
4. Freedman et al., (1976), p. 1328.
5. Webster (1968), p. 1321.
6. Freedman et al., (1976), p. 1328.
7. Webster (1968), p. 1322.
8. Drever, p. 262.
9. Webster (1968), p. 1322.
10. Hinsie & Campbell (1960), p.670.
11. Webster (1968), p. 1322.
12. Ibid., p. 1323.

Sensory. 'Relating to or conducting sensation.'[1]

Sensory/motor functions. Skill and performance patterns of sensory and motor behaviour that are prerequisites to self-care, work and play/leisure performance. Components are neuro-muscular and sensory integrative skills.

Skills. 'The abilities that a person has for the performance of various forms of purposeful behaviour.'[2]

Social interaction. 'Denotes the reciprocal influencing of the acts of persons in groups, usually mediated through communication. This definition includes the interaction of a person with himself. It may be defined operationally as what happens when people come into contact (not necessarily physical contact) and a modification of behaviour takes place.'[3]

Social isolation. See **Isolation**.

Socialization. The process by which society integrates the individual and the way in which the individual learns to become a functioning member of that society. 'In occupational therapy the term is applied to the development (in a patient) of those tendencies which induce him to be companionable and inclined to seek and mingle easily with a group.'[4]

Sociofugal. 'When the semi-fixed features of a room such as tables and chairs are arranged to discourage interaction.'[5]

Sociopetal. 'When the semi-fixed features of a room such as tables and chairs, are arranged to encourage interaction'[6]

Spontaneous. 'Of personal actions: arising or proceeding entirely from natural impulse; without any external stimulus or constraint; voluntary and of one's own accord.'[7]

Stimulation. See **Activation**.

Structured group. 'One in which the leaders structure the environment in an active and supportive way in order to ensure maximum participation of all members.'[8]

Subjective. 'Arising from within or belonging strictly to the individual . . .; arising out of or identified by means of an individual's attention to or awareness of his own states and processes.'[9]

Submission. 'The act of yielding to others; a type of behaviour on the part of an individual manifesting a tendency to submit to the dominance of others.'[10]

---

1. Faber, p. 397.
2. Kielhofner et al., (1985), p. 508.
3. Gould & Kolb, p. 657.
4. Hinsie & Campbell (1960), p. 681.
5. Bainhart, S. A., (1976) *Introduction to Interpersonal Communication*, p. 95. New York: Thomas Y. Crowell
6. Ibid.
7. *A New English Dictionary, Vol IX. Part 1. SI — ST* (1919), Murray, J. A. H., Bradley, H., Craigie. W. A. & Onions, C. T. (Eds.), p. 659. Oxford: Clarendon Press.
8. Kaplan, K. L. (1988) *Directive Group Therapy*. Thorofare, New Jersey: Slack.
9. Webster (1971), p. 2275.
10. Drever, p. 286.

Superego. 'In psychoanalytic theory, that part of the personality structure associated with ethics, standards and self-criticism. It is formed by the infant's identification with important and esteemed persons in his early life, particularly parents. The supposed or actual wishes of these significant persons are taken over as part of the child's own personal standards to help form the conscience.'[1] See **Ego** and **Id**.

Support, to. 'To actively promote the interests of . . . ; to give assistance to.'[2]

Supportive psychotherapy. 'A type of psychotherapy that aims to reinforce a patient's defences and to help him suppress disturbing psychological material. Supportive psychotherapy utilizes such measures as inspiration, reassurance, suggestion, persuasion, counselling and re-education. It avoids probing the patient's emotional conflicts in depth.'[3]

Suppression. 'The conscious effort to control and conceal unacceptable impulses, thoughts, feelings, or acts.'[4]

Symbolization. 'An unconscious mental process operating by association and based on similarity and abstract representation whereby one subject or idea comes to stand for another through some part, quality or aspect which the two have in common. The symbol carries in more or less disguised form the emotional feelings vested in the initial object or idea.'[5]

Sympathy. 'Compassion for another's grief or loss. To be differentiated from empathy.'[6]

Tactile. 'Relating to the sense of touch.'[7]

Temporal orientation. The degree to which a task is time-limiting or continuous, and seasonal or discretionary.[8]

Tension. 'An unpleasant alteration of affect characterized by a strenuous increase in mental and physical activity.'[9]

Theatre game. A simple, structured exercise, often used by actors to improve their abilities to think quickly, to be spontaneous, to improvise, to speak clearly, to trust others, to work in cooperation with others, to concentrate and to be decisive. The emphasis in a theatre game is upon clear, direct communication, whether it be verbal or nonverbal, and if it is used appropriately and in conjunction with other theatre games it can offer an excellent opportunity to practise, improve or change social behaviour in an enjoyable and accepting atmosphere.

---

1. Frazier, *et al.*, p. 143.
2. Webster (1917), p. 2297.
3. Frazier, *et al.*, p. 144.
4. Ibid.
5. Frazier, *et al.*, p. 144.
6. Ibid.
7. Faber, p. 430.
8. Kielhofner *et al.*, (1985), p. 509.
9. Freedman, *et al.*, (1976), p. 1333.

Therapeutic. 'Of or relating to the treatment of disease or disorders by remedial agents or methods.'[1]

Thinking. 'Any course or train of ideas; in the narrower and stricter sense, a course of ideas initiated by a problem.'[2]

Thinking, abstract. 'Thinking which is characterized by the use of abstractions and generalizations.'[3]

Thinking, concrete. The antithesis of abstract thinking. Concrete thinking is often associated with impairment of the frontal lobes. It is characterized by 'an inability to detach the ego from the inner and outer sphere of experience; an inability to concentrate on two tasks simultaneously; to integrate parts into a whole or to analyse a totality; and an inability to judge, reflect about or plan for the future.'[4]

Throughput. A person's ability to process information, based on the internal state of organization.

Tremor. 'Shaking or trembling. A disorder of muscular tone in which the usual, normal, unappreciable tonic contractions of a muscle become exaggerated to the point of awareness. In general, tremors can be classified into:

(1) coarse tremors, usually indicative of organic disease; included are —
  (a) passive or rest tremor, a tremor that occurs while the affected area is at rest, as the pill-rolling tremor of Parkinsonism;
  (b) action or intention tremor, which may be absent while the affected area is at rest and which is exaggerated by voluntary movement of the area, as the intention tremor of multiple sclerosis;

(2) fine tremors, often psychogenic, although they may also be on toxic basis (alcoholism, drug-poisoning hyperthyroidism, etc.);

(3) fasciculation, involuntary twitchings of a portion of a muscle; seen in fatigue, also in brain stem or anterior horn cell damage.'[5]

Trust, basic. 'S. Arieti (*Archives of General Psychiatry* 6, 122, 1962) emphasizes that basic trust is essential for the development of normal or satisfying relatedness.' 'Basic trust is an "atmospheric feeling" which predisposes one to expect "good things" and is prerequisite to a normal development of self-esteem....'[6]

Unconscious. 'That part of the mind or mental functioning of which the content is only rarely subject to awareness. It is the repository for data that have never been conscious (primary repression) or that may have become conscious briefly and later repressed (secondary repression.)'[7]

---

1. Webster (1971) p. 2372.
2. Drever, p. 298.
3. Wolman, p. 386.
4. Ibid.
5. Hinsie & Campbell (1970), p. 785.
6. Ibid., p. 658.
7. Frazier *et al.*, p. 149.

Values. 'Images of what is good, right and/or important.'[1]

Verbalization. 'In psychiatry, the state of being verbose or diffuse, commonly encountered in extreme degree in patients with the manic form of manic-depressive psychosis. In a more general sense, verbalization refers to the expression in words of thoughts, wishes, fantasies, or other psychic material which had previously been on a nonverbal level because of suppression. "Verbalize" is often used in a pseudoerudite way when "talk about" is meant.'[2]

Verbal technique. 'Any method of group or individual therapy in which words are used.'[3]

Videotape. 'A magnetic tape on which the electronic impulses of the video and audio portions of a television programme can be recorded for later broadcasting.'[4]

Volition sub-system. 'An interrelated set of energizing and symbolic components which together determine conscious choices for occupational behaviour.'[5]

Warm-up exercise. A technique, exercise or game of short duration used to promote an atmosphere in which individuals can begin to look at specific problems in general detail.

Withdrawal. 'The act of retracting, retiring, retreating or going away from. Withdrawal is used in psychiatry to refer to ... the turning away from objective, external reality ... the patient's retreat from society and interpersonal relationships into a world of his own.'[6] Often seen in schizophrenia and depression.

Word salad. 'A mixture of words and/or phrases which have no logical meaning. Commonly associated with schizophrenia.'[7]

REFERENCES

Curren, D., Partridge, M. & Storey, P. (1976) *Psychological Medicine: An Introduction to Psychiatry*. Edinburgh: Churchill Livingstone.

Freedman, A. M., Kaplan, H. I. & Sadock, B. J. (Eds.) (1975) *Comprehensive Textbook of Psychiatry*. Baltimore: Williams & Wilkins.

Freedman, A. M., Kaplan, H. I. & Sadock, B. J. (1976) *Modern Synopsis of Comprehensive Textbook of Psychiatry/II 2nd edn*. Baltimore: Williams & Wilkins.

Harrison, Randall R. (1974) *Beyond Words: An Introduction to Nonverbal Communication*. New Jersey: Prentice-Hall.

Leigh, D., Pare, C. M. B., Marks, J. (Eds.) (1977) *A Concise Encyclopaedia of Psychiatry*. Baltimore: University Park Press.

Kielhofner G. (Ed.) (1985) *A Model of Human Occupation, Theory and Application*. Baltimore: Williams & Wilkins.

1. Kielhofner *et al.*, (1985), p. 509.
2. Hinsie & Campbell (1970), p. 803.
3. Freedman *et al.*, (1972), p. 799.
4. Webster (1968), p. 1625.
5. Kielhofner *et al.*, (1985), p. 509.
6. Hinsie & Campbell (1970), p. 812.
7. Leigh *et al.*, p. 368.

Bibliography

This Bibliography offers some suggestions for supplementary reading; the books listed are taken from a wide variety of current publications. It invites you to both broaden your theoretical base and personal skills as well as sample a greater selection of nonverbal group techniques and their potential application.

Angel, S. L. (1981) *The emotion identification group.* American Journal of Occupational Therapy 35:256

Barris, R. (1982) *Environmental interactions: An extension of the model of occupation.* American Journal of Occupational Therapy 36:637

Brady, J. P. (1984) *Social skills training for psychiatric patients I: Concepts methods and clinical results.* Occupational Therapy in Mental Health 4:51

Brady, J. P. (1985) *Social skills training for psychiatric patients II: Clinical outcome studies.* Occupational Therapy in Mental Heath 5:59

Bruce, M., Borg, B (1987) *Frames of Reference in Psychosocial Occupational Therapy.* Thorofare, New Jersey: Charles B. Slack

Buck, R. E., Provancher, M. A. (1972) *Magazine picture collages as an evaluation technique.* American Journal of Occupational Therapy 26:36

Capon, S. (1975) *Perceptual Motor Development: Tire, Parachute Activities.* Belmont, CA: Fearon

Cynkin, S. (1979) *Occupational Therapy: Toward Health Through Activities.* Boston: Little, Brown

DeCarlo, J. J., Mann, W. C. (1985) *The effectiveness of verbal versus activity groups in improving self-perception of interpersonal communication skills.* American Journal of Occupational Therapy 39:20

Denton, P. L. (1982) *Teaching interpersonal skills with videotape.* Occupational Therapy in Mental Health 2:17

Denton, P. L. (1986) *Psychiatric Occupational Therapy: A Workbook of Practical Skills.* Boston: Little, Brown

Fluegelman, A. (1976) *The New Games Book.* San Francisco: The Headlands Press

Harrison, R. R. (1974) *Beyond Words: An Introduction to Nonverbal Communication.* New Jersey: Prentice Hall

Hertzman, M. (1984) *Inpatient Psychiatry: Toward Rapid Restoration of Function*. New York: Human Services Press

Kaplan, K. L. (1984) *Short-term assessment: The need and a response*. Occupational Therapy in Mental Health 4(3) pp. 29–45

Kaplan, K. L. (1988) *Directive Group Therapy: Innovative Mental Health Treatment*. New Jersey: Slack

Kielhofner, G. (Ed.) (1985) *A Model of Human Occupation: Theory and Application*. Baltimore: Williams & Wilkins

Lerner, C. (1982) *The Magazine Picture Collage*. In B. J. Hemphill (Ed.) *The Evaluative Process in Psychiatric Occupational Therapy*. Thorofare, New Jersey: Slack

Moriaty, J. (1976) *Combining activities and group psychotherapy in the treatment of chronic schizophrenia*. Hospital and Community Psychiatry 27, 574–576

Mosher, L., Keith, S. (1979) *Research on the psychosocial treatment of schizophrenia: A summary report*. American Journal of Psychiatry 136, 623–631

Smith, P. B. (1980) *Group Processes and Personal Change*. London: Harper & Row

Smith, P. B. (Ed.) (1980) *Small Groups and Personal Change*. London: Methuen

Vandenberg, B., Kielhofner, G., (1982) *Play in evolution, culture and individual adaptation: Implications for therapy*. American Journal of Occupational Therapy 36(I): 20-28

Yalom, I. (1983) *The Lower Level Psychotherapy Group: A Working Model*. Inpatient Group Psychotherapy. New York: Basic Books, pp. 275–312

Index

Entries in *italic* type indicate titles of exercises.
Entries in **bold** type indicate recognized problem areas.
Page numbers in **bold** type indicate glossary entries.